CGP GEOGRAPHY RESO[URCES]

GCSE GEOGRAPHY
The Essential Study Guide (OCR A)

This book perfectly covers the human and physical geography content for the OCR Examining Board, specification A.

The information is explained fully, and written concisely so that each topic can be displayed on a single page.

Contents

Section One
People & the Physical World

The Tectonic Jigsaw 1
Earthquakes 2
Volcanoes 3
Living with Tectonic Hazards 4
Case Studies 5
The Hydrological Cycle 6
Drainage Basins 7
Rivers and Valleys 8
Erosion, Transportation & Deposition 9
River Features of the Upper Stage 10
River Features of Middle & Lower Stages 11
Flooding — The Storm Hydrograph 12
Flood Control — Hard Engineering 13
Flood Control — Soft Engineering 14
Case Studies 15
The Power of the Sea 16
Coastal Landforms from Erosion 17
Coastal Landforms from Deposition 18
Erosion Control 19
Case Study 20
Revision Summary 21

Section Two
People & Places to Live

Population Distribution 23
Population Density 24
Population Structure 25
Population Dependency in LEDCs & MEDCs ... 26
Population Change 27
Managing Population Growth 28
Migration 29
Case Studies 30
Urbanisation 31
Urban Problems in LEDCs 32
Urban Land Use in MEDCs 33
Planning and the Rural-Urban Fringe 34
Improving the Urban Environment 35
The Settlement Hierarchy 36
Counter-Urbanisation 37
Case Studies 38
Revision Summary 40

Section Three
People and their Needs

Contrasts in Development 42
Measuring Development 43
Classification of Industry...................................... 44
Changing Industry — MEDCs 45
Changing Industry — LEDCs 46
Case Study 47
Classifying Farming 48
Distribution of Farming Types 49
Farming in the European Union (EU) 50
Location of Industry 52
Case Studies 54
The Leisure Industry 55
Tourism and LEDCs 56
Tourism and Conflict 57
Case Studies 58
Energy and Power 59
Effects of Changing Resources 60
Case Study 61
Revision Summary 62

Section Four
People & the Environment

Quarrying 64
Tropical Rainforests 65
Deforestation and Conservation 66
Sustainable Development in Forests 67
National Parks 68
Case Study 69
Pollution 70
Acid Rain 71
Global Warming 72
Case Study 73
Revision Summary 74

Section Five
Geographical Skills

Ordnance Survey Maps 76
Human Geography — Plans and Photos 78
Describing Maps and Charts 79
Types of Graphs and Charts 80
Revision Summary 85

Key Terms 87
Index 90

Published by CGP

Editors:
Kate Houghton
Becky May
Rachel Selway

Contributors:
Rosalind Browning, Martin Chester, Paul Cashman, Simon Cook,
Chris Dennett, Leigh Edwards, Dominic Hall, Tim Major,
Barbara Melbourne, Emma Singleton, James Paul Wallis.
Cover Design by David Rourke

With thanks to Edward Robinson and Eileen Worthington for proofreading.

The Tectonic Jigsaw

**Section One
People & the Physical World**

The Earth's crust is made of huge floating <u>plates</u>. It all sounds unlikely, but it's true and you need to <u>understand</u> it if you're going to get anywhere with <u>tectonics</u>.

The Earth's Crust is Divided up into <u>Plates</u>

<u>Plates</u> 'float' or move very slowly (a few mm per year) on the molten material of the <u>mantle</u> (the liquid insides of the Earth). This movement is caused by <u>convection currents</u> in the mantle. Plates meet at <u>plate boundaries</u> or <u>margins</u>.

There are <u>Three</u> Types of Plate Margin:

Divergent margins:

Two plates move away from each other.
Magma rises from the mantle.
New crust is created.

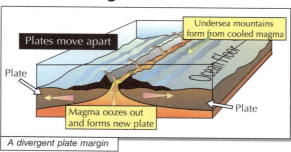
A divergent plate margin

Convergent margins:

Two plates move towards each other.
Crust is destroyed.
Fold mountains, earthquakes and volcanoes are common.

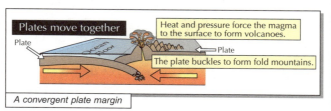
A convergent plate margin

FACT

The volcanoes under the sea at convergent boundaries can be so big that they eventually become islands. Iceland and Hawaii are good examples.

Transform margins:

Plates move sideways against each other.
Material isn't gained or lost.
Volcanoes are rare but earthquakes are common.

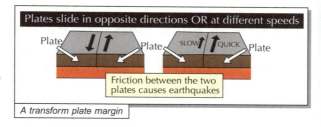
A transform plate margin

EXAMPLES

Plate Margins	Example
Divergent	Mid-Atlantic Ridge
Convergent	West coast of South America
Transform	San Andreas Fault (San Francisco)

Volcanoes and Earthquakes Occur <u>Near</u> Plate Margins

The two maps below show the main <u>plate boundaries</u> and where <u>volcanoes</u>, <u>earthquakes</u> and <u>fold mountains</u> are found. See how they match up — they are obviously connected because the patterns are very similar.

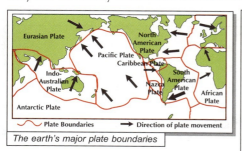
The earth's major plate boundaries

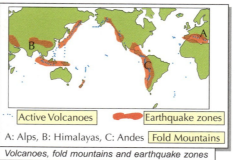
A: Alps, B: Himalayas, C: Andes
Volcanoes, fold mountains and earthquake zones

There are over 600 active volcanoes in the world today — the greatest concentration is around the Pacific Ocean, in the 'Ring of Fire'.

Section One — People & the Physical World

Earthquakes

Tectonic plates floating slowly around sounds fairly safe. But when the plates come together you can get earthquakes — which aren't so great...

EXAMPLES

Recent major earthquakes

Place	Year	Deaths	Size
Seattle	2001	0	7.2
India	2001	20,000	7.7
Turkey	1999	10,000	6.7
Kobe (Japan)	1995	5,000	7.2

Earthquakes Occur at Convergent or Transform Plate Margins

As two plates move towards each other, one can be pushed down under the other one and into the mantle. If this plate gets stuck it causes a lot of strain in the surrounding rocks. Sideways-moving plates can also get stuck.

When this tension in the rocks is finally released it produces strong shock waves known as seismic waves. This is called an earthquake.

The shock waves spread out from the focus — the point where the earthquake starts. Near the focus the waves are stronger and cause more damage.

The epicentre is the point on the Earth's surface immediately above the focus.

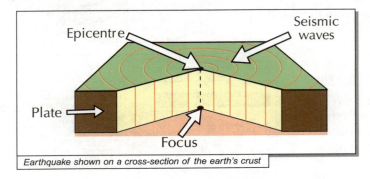

Earthquake shown on a cross-section of the earth's crust

EXAM TIP

The damage caused by an earthquake isn't just about the Richter Scale reading. It also depends on how strong the buildings are and how well people are prepared to deal with it.

The Richter Scale Measures Earthquakes

The size or magnitude of an earthquake is measured using a seismometer, a machine with a seismograph on a revolving drum. Earthquake vibrations are recorded by a sensitive arm with a pen at the end which moves up and down.

These readings are measured using the Richter Scale for energy released, which is an open-ended scale.

This is a logarithmic scale — which means, for example, that an earthquake with a score of 5 is ten times more powerful than one with a score of 4. One with a score of 4 is ten times more powerful than one that scores 3, and so on.

Most serious earthquakes are in the range of 5 to 9. The Richter Scale goes on forever but no earthquakes above 9 have ever been recorded.

EXAMPLE

The earthquake in San Francisco in 1906 was the most powerful in the last couple of centuries, with a value of 8.6.

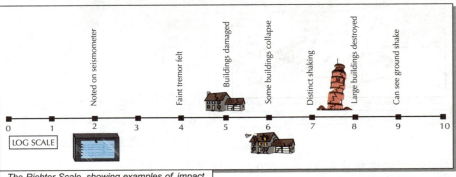

The Richter Scale, showing examples of impact

Volcanoes

**Section One
People & the Physical World**

Volcanoes are often (but not always) cone shaped, formed by material from the mantle being forced through an opening in the Earth's crust, the vent.

Volcanoes are Extinct, Dormant or Active

Volcanoes are split into three different categories depending on how likely they are to erupt.

Extinct volcanoes are those which will never erupt again.

Dormant volcanoes are those which haven't erupted for at least 2000 years. (Of course, just because a volcano is described as dormant, that doesn't mean it will never erupt again.)

Active volcanoes have erupted recently and are likely to erupt again.

EXAMPLES
Recent major eruptions

Major Active Volcanoes	
Place	Last Eruption
Mount Etna, Italy	2001
Montserrat, Caribbean	1997
Pinatubo, Phillipines	1991
Mount St. Helens, USA	1980

There are Three Main Types of Volcano

All volcanoes are caused by magma being forced out through the earth's crust at high pressure. The type of volcano depends on the composition and characteristics of the lava and ash that are extruded during the eruption.

A Composite Volcano is made up of Lava and Ash

Four different types of substance can be ejected through the vent: ash, gas, pieces of rock known as volcanic bombs, and molten rock. Molten rock is known as magma when it's under the ground, and lava when it reaches the surface.

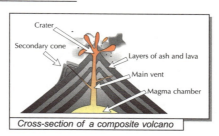
Cross-section of a composite volcano

Once this material has been thrown out at the surface, it cools and hardens, forming the volcano mountain from the mixture of ash and lava.

Shield volcanoes:
These are formed when the lava is basic (alkaline). This means it is runny and takes longer to cool and harden. The lava flows easily and spreads out to form wide, flat features.

Dome volcanoes:
These are formed when the lava is acidic (thicker). The lava flows slowly and hardens quickly forming steep-sided features.

EXAMPLES
Types of volcano:

Types of Volcano	
Volcano	Type
Mt. Etna, Sicily	Composite
Mauna Loa, Hawaii	Shield
Mt. St. Helens, USA	Dome

Volcanoes can have Positive or Negative Effects

Volcanoes have loads of different advantages and disadvantages:

Positive Effects	Negative Effects
Volcanoes create new land which can be used for farming or settlements.	People might be killed or injured during an eruption.
Lava soils are fertile, so crops grow well and yields are high.	Lava flows can damage infrastructure like roads and power supplies.
Local people gain employment if the volcano becomes a tourist attraction.	Farm animals and crops may be destroyed or damaged by lava and ash.
Geothermal energy can be used to generate electricity.	Ash and poisonous gases can cause serious respiratory illnesses.
Hot springs can be used for heating and hot water.	The cost of repairing damage can be very high.
	Volcanoes can trigger other hazards like fires and landslides.

Section One
People & the Physical World

Living With Tectonic Hazards

As well as knowing how earthquakes and volcanic eruptions ("tectonic hazards") occur, you also have to know how the hazards affect people, and how people try to cope with the dangers.

People Live in Earthquake and Volcanic Zones

You may find it hard to believe but millions of people live in places which could be devastated by tectonic hazards. Some people have no choice about where they live, and others just don't want to move. Even if everyone who lives in a tectonic zone wanted to leave, there'd be problems because more desirable areas are already over-crowded.

Some people live where there are tectonic hazards because they are confident that modern technology will enable scientists to predict hazards. They hope that they will have enough time to leave before an earthquake or eruption.

As well as the risks of living in tectonic areas there are quite a few benefits. For example, volcanic ash creates very fertile soils and geothermal energy can be used to heat homes, water and greenhouses. Tourists are often interested to see the effects of volcanoes and earthquakes so hazards can be important sources of income for some regions.

> **EXAM TIP**
> If you are asked about the advantages and disadvantages of living where there are tectonic hazards, make sure you write a balanced answer that shows you understand both arguments.

> **EXAM TIP**
> There's more about the pros and cons of living with volcanoes on page 3.

Scientists Try to Predict Hazards in Advance

It's possible to monitor the tell-tale signs that precede a volcanic eruption. Things such as tiny earthquakes, rising magma, escaping gas, increased magma temperature and changes in the tilt of volcano sides all mean an eruption is likely.

Earthquakes are harder to predict but there are some clues like changes in well water levels, gas emissions, new cracks in rocks, and strange animal behaviour.

Computers are used to analyse past data to forecast future eruptions and earthquakes.

Good Planning Reduces the Effects of a Hazard

- Monitoring helps predict when hazards are coming so people can be warned.
- Families can organise supplies of food and water rations, dust masks, spare clothes, basic medical supplies, shelters, torches, batteries, mobile phones and other useful items.
- Local emergency services such as the police, fire brigade and ambulance service can be well prepared to deal with any hazard.
- Information on emergency procedures can be made available to the public — e.g. in school classes, meetings for adults, leaflets, newspaper adverts etc. Simply sheltering under a table or avoiding standing next to walls can save someone's life.
- Emergency supplies of water and power can be organised in advance.
- Buildings and roads can be designed to cope with earth movements, so they don't collapse under the strain. For example, new skyscrapers in earthquake zones can be built with a computer controlled counterweight, cross-bracings and special foundations to reduce the impact of an earthquake.

> **EXAMPLE**
> Strengthening roads and railways doesn't always help reduce damage. For example, in the 1995 Kobe earthquake the Bullet Traintrack bent unexpectedly.

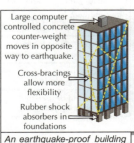

Large computer controlled concrete counter-weight moves in opposite way to earthquake.
Cross-bracings allow more flexibility
Rubber shock absorbers in foundations

An earthquake-proof building

Case Studies

**Section One
People & the Physical World**

It's really important that you're able to show your understanding of plate tectonics by using real-life examples. In this section you must show an understanding of the causes and effects of a volcanic eruption and an earthquake.

Case Study 1: Mount St. Helens Volcanic Eruption, 1980

Mount St. Helens is a volcanic mountain in the Cascade Range in the state of Washington, USA. This area has a long history of volcanic activity and Mount St. Helens has been the most active volcano in the area for the last 4000 years.

Before it erupted in 1980, Mount St. Helens hadn't erupted for 123 years.

Scientists carefully monitored the volcano before the 1980 eruption but they still couldn't predict exactly when the volcano would erupt. In the days before the eruption there were a number of small earthquakes and mini-eruptions.

Scientists monitoring Mt St Helens

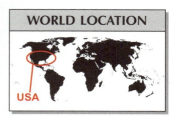
WORLD LOCATION

The eruption began with an earthquake measuring 5 on the Richter Scale. Pressurised magma exploded through the side of the mountain. The explosion was 500 times stronger than the atomic bomb used on Hiroshima.

Ice and snow on the mountain melted and caused fast flowing mudflows. The mudflows picked up cars, trees and even whole buildings.

Ash from the eruption was thrown high into the atmosphere and travelled around the earth in the following weeks.

Fortunately, the area is sparsely populated. There was enough warning to evacuate and close the area, which saved many lives.

USA LOCATION

Case Study 2: Earthquake in Kobe, 1995

Kobe is a city in Japan that's located close to a convergent margin between three tectonic plates. In 1995 an earthquake measuring 7.2 on the Richter Scale happened. The epicentre of the earthquake was under the sea in Osaka Bay.

Damaged road systems in Kobe

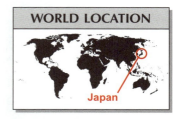
WORLD LOCATION

Over 5000 people were killed and thousands were injured. Many buildings including houses and schools collapsed, and roads and railways were damaged. Lots of fires started because of broken gas pipes and electrical cables. The damage to the transport systems meant it was difficult for the emergency services to get to the fires and to injured people.

Immediately after the earthquake emergency shelters were set up and food and water were brought in. The lack of clean water vastly increased the risk of disease. The clearing of rubble took many months and the re-building of homes, schools, businesses and infrastructure like railways took years.

New laws, building codes and emergency plans have been brought in since 1995 to reduce devastation if there is another earthquake. The amount of monitoring equipment in the area has been increased to try and predict future earthquakes.

JAPANESE LOCATION

Section One
People & the Physical World

The Hydrological Cycle

The hydrological cycle is the movement of a constant amount of water between the sea, land and atmosphere. It's a continuous cycle with no start or end point.

Evaporated Sea Water Forms the *Inputs* to the System

Clouds of evaporated sea water blow towards land where they rise, causing precipitation like rain, snow or hail to fall on the ground below.

Then the Water *Flows* Through the System via *Transfers*

There are two kinds of transfer to learn about — vertical and horizontal.

Vertical Transfers:
Water collects on plant leaves — this is called interception. Then it drips off and enters the soil. It can then filter through the soil through spaces in the surface layers — this is called infiltration. Infiltrated water can also move downwards vertically, into the deeper layers — this is called percolation.

Horizontal Transfers:
There are four kinds of horizontal transfer that you need to know about:
- Surface run-off is when water flows overground to rivers, lakes or the sea.
- Channel flow is the flow of water in a stream, river or lake.
- Through flow is when infiltrated water moves through soil to a river.
- Groundwater flow is when percolated water moves below the water table to a river.

EXAM TIP

The water cycle is really important — you'll definitely need it for the next nine pages and it'll help with loads of other topics in the book.

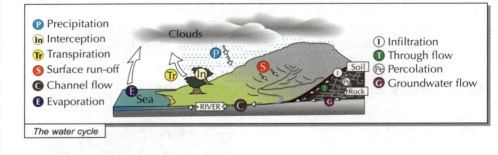

The water cycle

Some Water is *Stored* in the System

There are four kinds of storage that you need to know about:
- Channel storage happens in rivers and lakes and is vital for our water supply.
- Groundwater storage occurs in underground rocks which are porous. This means they collect water in the pores, which are spaces between their particles. The water table is the upper surface of saturated rocks in an area.
- Soil water storage is when water is stored in the soil and is used by plants.
- Short-term shortage occurs after interception on things like plant leaves and in puddles.

KEY TERM

A water-carrying rock is known as an aquifer. An example of an aquifer is chalk.

Evaporated Water is the *Output*

There are three ways that water can get back into the atmosphere:
- Evaporation happens when sea, lake or river water is heated by the sun. The water vapour rises, then cools and condenses to form clouds.
- Transpiration is when plants lose moisture.
- Evapotranspiration is both evaporation and transpiration together.

Drainage Basins

**Section One
People & the Physical World**

All rivers have their own drainage basin.

A *Drainage Basin* is a Land Area Drained by a River

Catchment area and drainage basin mean the same thing — the land area from which a river and its tributaries collect the rainwater passing from the soil and rock. The land provides the water source for the main river and all its tributaries.

The size of the catchment area depends on the size of the river. A watershed is high ground separating two neighbouring drainage basins. On one side of the watershed the water drains in one direction, and on the other side it drains the opposite way.

FACT

Drainage basins can be vast. For example, the Amazon drainage basin covers most of Brazil. In combination the Ganges and Brahmaputra rivers drain an area six times the size of Britain.

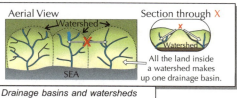
Drainage basins and watersheds

A Drainage Basin Works as a *System*

Water enters the drainage basin as precipitation. It goes through a series of flows and stores before reaching the sea as river run-off. The time between rain and river run-off depends on the characteristics of the basin — e.g. its shape, size, rock type and vegetation.

Energy is put into the system by the steepness of the hills / valley and the force of gravity. Water moves rock and soil material through the drainage basin system. It's picked up when the water energy is high and deposited when energy is low.

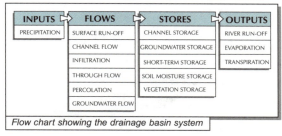
Flow chart showing the drainage basin system

A River Basin has Several Important *Features*

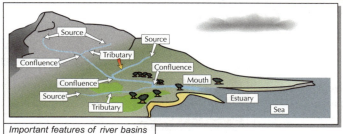
Important features of river basins

- The source is where a river starts, usually in an upland area.
- A tributary is a stream or smaller river that joins the main river.
- A confluence is the point where two rivers join.
- The mouth is where the river flows into the sea.
- An estuary is where the mouth is low enough to let sea enter at high tide. This causes deposition, forming mud banks, which the river flows between.

EXAM TIP

Using the correct terms to describe drainage basins will save time in the exam and impress the examiners.

Section One
People & the Physical World

Rivers and Valleys

The different stages of a river's course each have their own characteristics.

Rivers Flow in Linear Features called Valleys

A <u>river</u> flows from an <u>upland source</u> to the <u>mouth</u> where it enters the sea. The river channel <u>widens</u> as it follows its course to the sea, and the <u>amount</u> of water it carries (its <u>discharge</u>) increases as <u>other</u> streams and rivers <u>join it</u>.

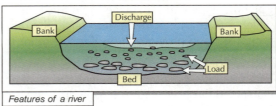
Features of a river

High <u>velocity</u> (the speed of flow in one direction) results in high <u>energy</u> — e.g. during floods or when the river's gradient is steep. Rivers with lots of energy wear away the <u>channel banks</u>, producing the <u>load</u> — sand and stones. When a river has little energy, the load is <u>deposited</u> on the <u>bed</u> and <u>banks</u>.

A Valley Cross Profile has Three Stages

<u>Upper</u>: near the source it is V-shaped — it has a <u>narrow floor</u> and <u>steep sides</u>.
<u>Middle</u>: lower down the river, the <u>floor</u> is <u>wider</u> and <u>sides</u> are more <u>gently sloping</u>.
<u>Lower</u>: near to the sea, the river has a <u>wide floor</u> and <u>gentle sides</u>.

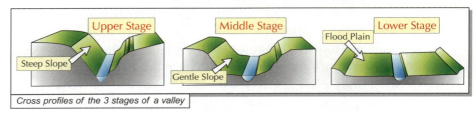
Cross profiles of the 3 stages of a valley

A River's Long Profile Varies as it Moves Downstream

In the <u>upper</u> stage, the river's gradient is quite <u>steep</u>.

In the <u>middle</u> stage it's <u>more gentle</u>.

In the <u>lower</u> stage it's <u>very gentle</u> and almost <u>flat</u>.

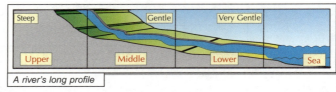
A river's long profile

Erosion is When the River Wears Land Away

Rivers erode in four main ways, called <u>erosion processes</u>:

<u>Corrasion</u> or <u>abrasion</u> is when large pieces of <u>bedload</u> material wear away the riverbed and banks — e.g. in floods. If material collects in a dip, it swirls around forming a <u>pothole</u>.

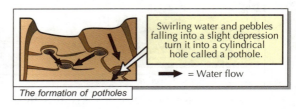
The formation of potholes

<u>Attrition</u> means rocks being transported are <u>eroded</u>. <u>Sediment particles</u> knock against the bed or each other and <u>break apart</u>, becoming smaller and more round.

<u>Hydraulic action</u> is when the <u>force</u> of the water wears away at softer rocks such as clay. It can also <u>weaken</u> rocks along bedding planes and joints.

<u>Solution</u> or <u>corrosion</u> is when chalk and limestone <u>dissolve</u> in water.

SUMMARY

River cross profile

Stage	Floor	Sides
Upper	Narrow	Steep
Middle	Wide	Gently sloping
Lower	Very wide	Gentle

River long profile

Stage	Gradient
Upper	Steep
Middle	More gentle
Lower	Very gentle, almost flat

KEY TERM

Bedload — rocks plucked from river banks and carried along at the bottom of the river.

SUMMARY

Four types of erosion:
- corrasion
- attrition
- hydraulic action
- solution

Erosion, Transportation & Deposition

**Section One
People & the Physical World**

The ways that a river shapes the landscape can be grouped into three categories — erosion (removing), transportation (moving) and deposition (leaving behind).

River Erosion is Headward, Vertical or Lateral

Headward erosion is when the furthest point upstream, the valley head, is worn away by rainwash, undercutting or soil creep (the slow movement of soil downhill over time).

Vertical erosion deepens the valley as the water force grows — common in the upper stage when the gradient is steep.

Lateral erosion widens the valley, combined with weathering of the sides — it's common in middle and lower stage valleys.

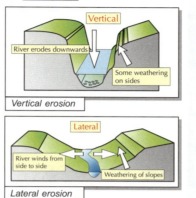

SUMMARY	
River Erosion	
Type	Description
Headward Erosion	Wears away the valley head
Vertical Erosion	Deepens the valley
Lateral Erosion	Widens the valley

Transportation is the Movement of Eroded Material

A river transports its load downstream in four ways:
- **Suspension** is when fine silt and clay material is carried along in the water.
- **Saltation** is when small sand-sized particles are bounced along the riverbed.
- **Traction** — larger materials like boulders are dragged along the bed.
- **Solution** is when eroded material dissolved in the water is carried away.

EXAM TIP

Learn these diagrams so you can draw them from memory. It will save you time in the exam as there will be less text to write.

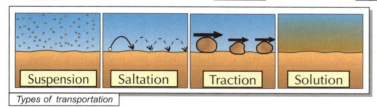
Types of transportation

Deposition is When a River Dumps its Load

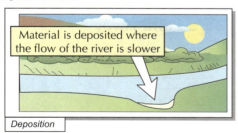
Deposition

It can happen when the velocity is lower than normal and the river can't move as much material.

It also happens when a river's load is increased — e.g. after a landslide.

Deposition can form deltas where rivers enter a sea or lake.

EXAMPLE

The large natural levees on the Mississippi River are a good example of depositional river features.

There are Four Stages of Deposition

- Large material carried by the river is deposited in the higher reaches.
- Gravel, sand and silt, carried as bedload or in suspension, are laid down in the lower reaches.
- Fine particles of suspended silt and clay are laid down in estuaries and deltas.
- Dissolved load is not deposited, but stays in solution and is carried out to sea.

**Section One
People & the Physical World**

River Features of the Upper Stage

Many of the more notable and dramatic river features are found at the upper stage.

Interlocking Spurs are Caused by Erosion

In its upper stage the river erodes vertically rather than laterally.

Interlocking spurs are ridges produced when a river in the upper stage twists and turns round obstacles of hard rock along its downward pathway.

These ridges interlock with one another like the teeth of a zip fastener.

EXAMPLE

Interlocking spurs are found in the upper stages of many British rivers, such as the River Ouse in Yorkshire.

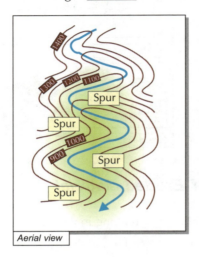
Aerial view

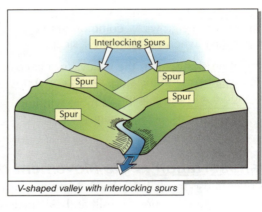
V-shaped valley with interlocking spurs

Waterfalls are Found at Steep Parts of the River Bed

A layer of hard rock won't erode very easily so when the river reaches it, any softer rocks on the downstream side are eroded more quickly. This means the river bed gets steeper where it crosses the hard rocks and a waterfall forms.

Waterfalls can form when the hard rock is horizontal, vertical or dips upstream (rock slopes down as you go upstream). At the foot of the waterfall the water wears away the softer rock to form a plunge pool.

As the waterfall retreats and eats its way upstream, a recessional gorge is formed.

EXAMPLE

Niagara Falls, on the American-Canadian border

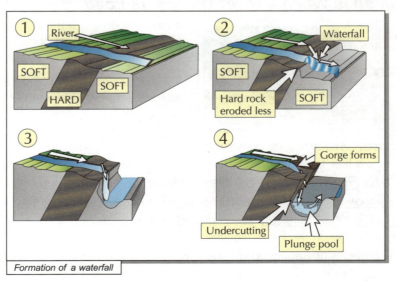
Formation of a waterfall

River Features of Middle & Lower Stages

Section One — People & the Physical World

Middle and lower stage river features are often more temporary and changeable than upper stage features.

The Middle and Lower Stages have Meanders

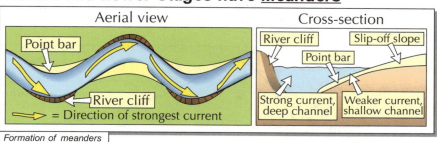
Formation of meanders

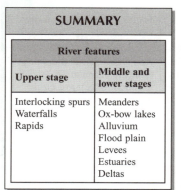

SUMMARY

River features	
Upper stage	**Middle and lower stages**
Interlocking spurs	Meanders
Waterfalls	Ox-bow lakes
Rapids	Alluvium
	Flood plain
	Levees
	Estuaries
	Deltas

The river now has a <u>large discharge</u>, <u>gentle gradient</u> and <u>lateral erosion</u>. It develops a more winding pathway with <u>large bends</u> — these bends are called <u>meanders</u>.

The river twists — over time the course of the meander migrates <u>downstream</u>. The current is <u>fastest</u> on the <u>outside</u> of the meander curve, causing greater erosion here so the channel becomes <u>deeper</u>. On the <u>inside</u> the <u>slower</u> current causes <u>deposition</u> — making this area more <u>shallow</u>.

<u>River cliffs</u> are found on the meander's <u>outer edge</u> where the river causes more erosion. <u>Point bars</u> are on the <u>inner edge</u> where sandy material is <u>deposited</u> by the slower-moving river — above river level they're <u>slip-off slopes</u>.

Ox-Bow Lakes are Formed from Wide Meander Loops

<u>Meander loops</u> can become so <u>sinuous</u> (wavy) that the river's easiest path is <u>straight across</u>, so it breaks through the narrow <u>neck of land</u> in between.

The <u>outer part</u> of the loop is left <u>isolated</u> from the river as an <u>ox-bow lake</u>.

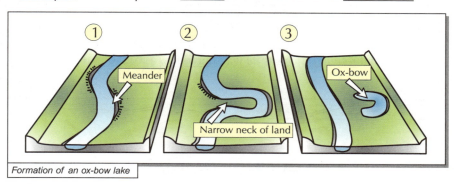
Formation of an ox-bow lake

FACT

Large rivers like the Amazon have many large meanders and ox-bow lakes. They are often short-term features — e.g. ox-bow lakes are gradually taken over by plants, dry up and become marshes.

The Lower Stage has Several Important Features

The river now has its greatest discharge — it has a really big cross-sectional area.

- The <u>flood plain</u> is the <u>wide valley floor</u> which the river regularly floods. It's <u>flat</u> and covered by alluvium, making it <u>good farmland</u>.
- <u>Levees</u> are <u>raised river banks</u>, made of coarse river load material deposited during <u>floods</u>.

Flooding — The Storm Hydrograph

Hydrographs are used to study the flow of rivers and predict when floods are likely.

Using the Storm Hydrograph

The graph shows the change in river discharge (volume of water flowing per second) over a short period of time after a storm. It's used to work out when a flood might be coming.

TIP

Remember, river discharge is always measured in cumecs, which are cubic metres per second.

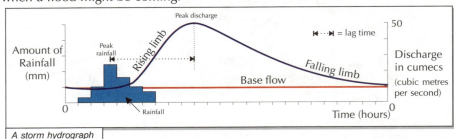

A storm hydrograph

- The base flow is the normal discharge of the river.
- The rising limb represents the increase in discharge after the storm.
- The falling or recession limb represents the decrease in discharge.
- The lag time is the amount of time between peak rainfall and peak discharge.

The river is likely to flood when the graph is steep. This is because there is a rapid increase in discharge over a short period of time — the river system is unable to transport it away before it floods onto the surrounding land.

FACT

There is always a delay between peak rainfall and peak flow because it takes a while for all the water that falls in the drainage basin to get into the river channel.

Several Factors Affect the Steepness of the Graph

The steeper the graph, the more likely the river is to flood:

FACTOR	STEEPER ⋀	GENTLER ⌒
1. Total Rainfall	High	Low
2. Intensity of Rain	High (runs off)	Low (soaks in)
3. Wetness of Ground	Saturated (runs off)	Dry (soaks in)
4. Rock Type	Impermeable (runs off)	Porous (soaks in)
5. Ground Cover	Bare Soil (runs off)	Vegetated (soaks in)
6. Slope Angle	Steep (runs quickly)	Gentle (runs slowly)

Factors which affect the shape of the hydrograph

FACT

Increased vegetation leads to a gentler graph because some of the water is intercepted by vegetation, which prevents it getting into the river channel.

Floods can Cause Extensive Damage

The amount of damage caused by a flood depends on where it happens, how severe it is and how well prepared people are to deal with it. Floods can cause extensive damage and disruption because they affect many different things:

The impact of flooding

Flood Control — Hard Engineering

**Section One
People & the Physical World**

Hard engineering involves building structures like dams to control the river system.

Dams can Control Discharge for a Whole Valley

Dams and reservoirs in the upper parts of a drainage basin are very effective for controlling the discharge lower down the valley — where the flood threat is greatest. Dams are expensive to build so recently multi-purpose schemes have been built, including hydro-electric power (HEP) stations and recreational lakes — e.g. at Kielder in Northumberland.

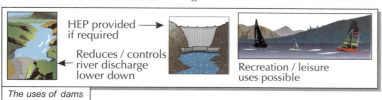

The uses of dams

The Hoover Dam, Nevada, USA

The Hoover Dam has several different purposes:
- Controlling the flow of the river
- Water storage
- HEP
- Recreation
- Tourism

The disadvantage of such schemes is that countryside can be spoiled by ugly buildings and farmland can be destroyed when upper valley floors are flooded.

All the river sediment is deposited in the reservoir instead of on the floodplain downstream. This means the floodplain is less fertile, forcing the farmers to use more fertiliser. Also, coastal beaches and deltas (flat areas of alluvial deposition where some rivers join the sea) lose their sediment.

The sediment-free water released by the dam increases erosion downstream. This increases the river width, causing problems for bridges and river-side buildings.

The River's Shape can be Changed to Control Flooding

Increasing the capacity of the channel means it can hold more water in a flood.

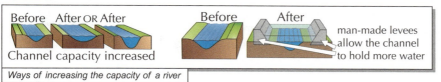

Ways of increasing the capacity of a river

Culverts straighten and line the river channel to increase the speed of the river and remove excess water more quickly down the channel to the sea.

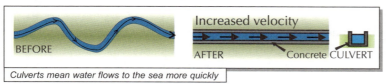

Culverts mean water flows to the sea more quickly

Straightening river channels means that they carry water away from areas that are at risk from flooding quickly.

Building branching channels off the main river removes the excess water by:
- Taking water to a neighbouring basin with a cut-through.
- Diverting extra water into storage areas on the flood plain.
- Building relief channels round towns to hold the excess water.

Artificial Changes to River Channels Cause Problems

- Channels need regular dredging to stop the channel size decreasing.
- Increased channel speed causes flooding and erosion downstream.
- The engineering often looks ugly and affects the natural river ecosystems.
- If a dam, levee or cut-through breaks there could be a big, sudden disaster.

Section One
People & the Physical World

Flood Control — Soft Engineering

To avoid the disadvantages of hard engineering, water authorities are moving to more sustainable flood controls, using 'soft engineering'. Instead of trying to control rivers, soft engineering works by using natural drainage basin processes to reduce flooding.

Prediction — Spotting Problems Before they Happen

Soft engineering relies on detailed research into drainage basin systems to work out how to solve one flood problem without causing new ones. To find out if an area is in danger of flooding, the whole drainage basin is looked at. Scientists assess the geology, soil, drainage and precipitation characteristics of the drainage basin.

They also investigate the human activities in the basin to make sure they've got a good overview of all the factors which affect channel flow in the basin. Another way of finding out when floods are likely to happen is to look for patterns in the flood-history data for the river.

Changing Land Use can help Reduce Flooding

One of the easiest 'soft engineering' ways of avoiding flood problems is not to build houses where it floods. But... many people already live in flood zones and they're not leaving, so different strategies are needed.

> **EXAM TIP**
> Remember soft engineering is really popular in geography at the moment because it is more sustainable than hard engineering. It's worth learning because it comes up in the coasts section too (see page 19).

Afforestation of bare slopes in the upper reaches reduces run-off as trees intercept the rain. Lag time is longer — with less run-off or river discharge.

Leaving land upstream as pasture gives continuous plant cover, which reduces run-off as more water is intercepted by plants. It's better than using land for growing crops, which leaves soil bare and open to run-off during the non-growing season.

Man-made surfaces, such as concrete, allow rapid run-off. Plants and grass areas can be used instead to reduce flooding in urban areas.

Traditional man-made drainage systems use fast draining pipes leading directly into watercourses causing floods. Sustainable Urban Drainage Systems (SUDS) reduce the flow and amount of urban drainage by directing rainwater into the soil, slow draining channels or ponds.

LEDCs are lagging behind — soft engineering is predominantly used in MEDCs where there's more money available to invest in flood prediction, prevention and control.

Soft engineering methods
- Afforestation
- Pasture land
- Plants and grass areas in towns
- Sustainable Urban Drainage Systems (SUDS)

> **TIP**
> See page 72 for more about global warming.

Things *Aren't* Getting any Better

Scientists believe that the severe flooding we've had in recent years could be an effect of global warming. If this is true, flood control will be even more important in the future.

Flooding could become more common

Case Studies

Section One
People & the Physical World

It's important that you're able to demonstrate your knowledge of the effects of flooding in MEDCs and in LEDCs. Generally flooding affects LEDCs more, but MEDCs are also vulnerable.

Case Study 1: Flooding in Bangladesh, 1988 (LEDC)

Much of Bangladesh lies on a huge flood plain on the delta of two large rivers — the Ganges and the Brahmaputra. It is a very poor country so there is little money available to minimise the problems caused by floods.

Human causes
- The flatter, lower lying valleys are built up and heavily populated.
- Urbanisation increased the risk of flooding because surface run-off was increased over the concrete surfaces.
- Deforestation reduced interception rates and infiltration. This in turn increased the risk of flooding.

Physical causes
- Monsoon rains caused the ground to become saturated quickly.
- Snowmelt from the Himalayas added to the volume of water.
- Tropical cyclones and storms caused heavy rain and worsened conditions for rescue.
- Flat land in the area became flooded quickly — a lot of the land is less than 1m above sea-level.

Impact of flooding
- 2000 people killed
- 7 million homes destroyed
- 25 million people made homeless
- food supplies destroyed, leading to starvation and health problems

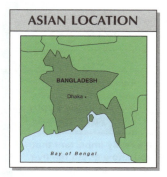

Case Study 2: Flooding in the UK, 2000 (MEDC)

During October and November of 2000, large scale flooding occurred across the British Isles. The floods were caused by a series of deep depressions from the Atlantic Ocean. Some scientists believe extreme weather like this is caused by global warming.

One of the worst-hit areas was Yorkshire, especially York and Selby.

The River Ouse burst its banks in York and hundreds of buildings were flooded. Millions of pounds of damage was caused and 3000 people were left homeless.

Flooding in York

To try and reduce damage, thousands of sandbags were filled, distributed and stacked up against doorways. The emergency services and the army helped to evacuate people stranded in their homes. Churches and sports halls were used as temporary housing.

Unlike Bangladesh, the UK can afford to take measures to reduce the effects of flooding. After the York floods the Deputy Prime Minister, John Prescott, pledged £51 million for improving flood defences. Environmentalists argued that this money should be spent on planting trees to increase interception of precipitation.

Section One — People & the Physical World

The Power of the Sea

Waves are energy movements through water caused by the wind — they're the main way in which the sea erodes, transports and deposits material.

Waves can be Constructive or Destructive

FACT
Constructive and destructive waves have big effects on the coasts. Constructive waves deposit material like sand and shingle to form beaches. Destructive waves take material way and cause a lot of erosion.

- Constructive waves operate in calmer weather and are about a metre high. The swash is strong and erosion is limited. They're involved with the transport and deposition of material, creating landforms.
- Destructive waves operate in storm conditions and are about 5 or 6 metres high. The backwash is strong and there is a lot of erosion.

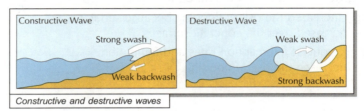
Constructive and destructive waves

The Sea Erodes the Coast in Five Ways

Hydraulic action: lots of sea water crashes against the land, and air and water are trapped and compressed in rock surface cracks. When the sea moves away again the air expands explosively, weakening the rocks, enlarging the cracks and breaking pieces off.

Corrasion (abrasion) is very effective and is caused by broken rock fragments battering the land and cliffs and breaking off other pieces of rock.

Attrition occurs when rock fragments grind each other down into smaller and smoother pebbles, shingle, and finally sand which is later deposited as beaches.

Corrosion involves chemical action of sea on rock. If the rock is limestone, it dissolves in the sea-water — some sea salts can also react with certain rocks and cause them to rot.

Wave pounding is the 'battering ram' action of the weight of the pounding waves.

EXAM TIP
It's really important that you know about the five types of erosion — they're relevant for most questions that you could get on coasts. Don't worry if it takes you a while to learn them though — it's difficult because corrasion, corrosion and attrition all sound fairly similar.

Waves can Move Material along the Coast

Longshore drift happens when waves break at an oblique angle to the shore (not right angles) due to the prevailing wind.

This means that each wave pushes material along the beach a bit more.

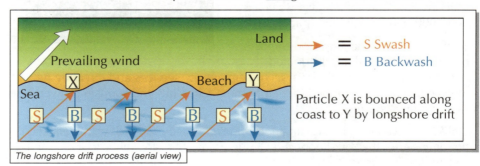
The longshore drift process (aerial view)

Coastal Landforms from Erosion

**Section One
People & the Physical World**

Wave erosion forms many coastal features over long periods of time.

Rock Erosion Forms Cliffs

Waves erode rocks along the shoreline by hydraulic action, corrosion, corrasion, solution and pounding. A notch is slowly formed at the high water mark which may develop into a cave. Rock above the notch becomes unstable with nothing to support it, and it eventually collapses.

The coastline can retreat over many years as this process continues to form a wave cut platform with cliffs behind. The actual size and angle of the cliff will depend on the local rock and its hardness, etc.

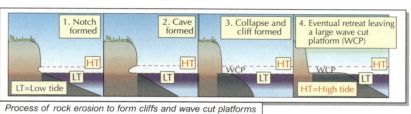
Process of rock erosion to form cliffs and wave cut platforms

Eroded Hard and Soft Rocks form Headlands

If there are alternate bands of hard and softer rock in the coastline, the harder rocks take longer to erode than the softer rocks — because the sea has less effect.

The hard rock will be left jutting out, forming one or more headlands — usually with cliffs. The softer rock will be eroded to form bays — the erosion means that the bays will usually slope more gently inland, creating room for a beach to form.

Again, the local geology will affect the actual shape and size of the features formed.

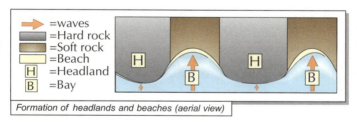
Formation of headlands and beaches (aerial view)

Caves, Arches and Stacks can also be Formed

A crack or rock weakness in a headland can be eroded — wave energy is usually strong there because the headland juts out. This forms one or more caves.

Occasionally the pressure of air, compressed in the caves by the waves, weakens the roof along a major joint and the rock collapses to form a blow hole. Further erosion enlarges the cave and it breaks through the headland, forming an arch.

The roof of this arch is often unstable and eventually collapses leaving a stack or series of stacks.

Areas with a limestone or chalk geology are prone to this kind of erosion.

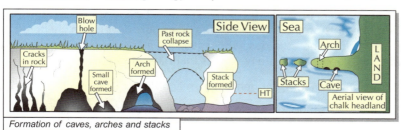
Formation of caves, arches and stacks

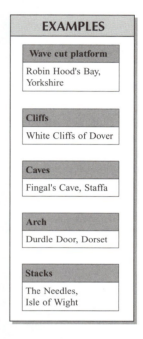

EXAMPLES
Wave cut platform
Robin Hood's Bay, Yorkshire
Cliffs
White Cliffs of Dover
Caves
Fingal's Cave, Staffa
Arch
Durdle Door, Dorset
Stacks
The Needles, Isle of Wight

Section One — People & the Physical World

Coastal Landforms from Deposition

Deposition forms specific coastal features.

Beaches are Formed by *Deposition*

Beaches are found on coastlines where eroded material in the sea has been deposited — e.g. in bays between headlands. They vary in size from tiny Cornish inlets to vast stretches, like at Blackpool. Beach fragment size depends on local rock type and wave energy.

Storm beaches are ridges of boulders at the landward side of beaches caused by heavy seas piling up material at the high-tide mark.

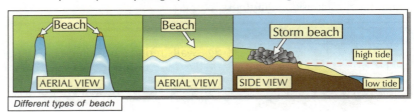
Different types of beach

TIP
There's more about longshore drift on page 16.

Spits are Long Beaches formed by *Longshore Drift*

Spits are sand or pebble beaches sticking out to sea, but joined to the land at one end — they are mainly formed by the process of longshore drift.

Spits tend to be formed across river mouths, where the coast suddenly changes direction, or where tides meet calmer waters of a bay or inlet.

At the spit end there are usually some hooks (also called recurves) formed by occasional strong winds from another direction. Waves can't reach the sea areas behind the spit, so they're often mud flats and salt marshes.

Formation of a mature spit

EXAMPLES

Fine sand beach
Blackpool

Pebble beach
Hastings

Spits
Mouth of River Exe, Devon

Orford Ness, Suffolk

Tombolo
Chesil beach, south coast

Bar
Slapton Ley, S. Devon

Tombolos and *Bars* Join bits of Land together

Tombolos are found where an island is joined to the mainland by a ridge of deposited material, e.g. Chesil Beach on the south coast — this is 18km long and joins the Isle of Portland to the mainland.

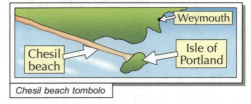
Chesil beach tombolo

Bars are barriers of sand which stretch across bays and connect to two different points on the mainland. They can only develop in sheltered bays where there are no estuaries. The water that gets trapped behind a bar is called a lagoon. There are two ways that bars can form:

- If a spit grows long enough it may reach the far side of a bay creating a bar.
- Sometimes sandbars develop off the shore. These can be moved in towards the shore by the tides so that they cross a bay.

Erosion Control

**Section One
People & the Physical World**

There are two different kinds of approach to defending against coastal erosion — <u>hard</u> and <u>soft</u> engineering.

There are <u>Five</u> Main <u>Hard Engineering</u> Defences

- Groynes are wooden structures placed at right angles to the coast where longshore drift occurs. They <u>reduce</u> movement of material along the coast, and <u>hold</u> the beach in place — <u>protecting</u> the cliff from further erosion in some parts. The beach will then <u>protect</u> low areas.

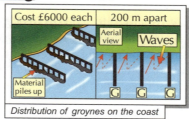
Distribution of groynes on the coast

EXAMPLES
Groynes
Bournemouth
Sea wall
Scarborough
Armour blocks
Barton-on-Sea

Sea wall

- Sea walls reduce erosion — but they <u>deflect</u> (not absorb) waves, so waves can still <u>wash away</u> the protective beach. The waves also <u>erode</u> the wall itself which can collapse.

- Revetments (slatted barriers) are built where a sea wall would be <u>too expensive</u>, e.g. out of towns. They <u>break</u> the wave force, trapping beach material behind them and <u>protecting</u> the cliff base — they're <u>cheaper</u> than sea walls but look unattractive and <u>don't</u> give full protection.

- Gabions are steel mesh cages containing boulders, built onto the cliff face above a sea wall. The rocks <u>absorb</u> some of the wave energy and <u>cut down</u> erosion — they're cheap but ugly.

- Armour blocks are large boulders piled on beaches where erosion is likely. They're cheap but ugly and they can be <u>moved by waves</u>.

FACT

Hard engineering style sea defences are not sustainable in the long term. They are expensive, unattractive, need constant maintenance and often cause problems further down the coast. Tourism can suffer where hard defences are used because they make the environment less pleasant.

A More <u>Sustainable</u> Approach — <u>Soft Engineering</u>

The easiest <u>soft engineering</u> option is to leave the sea to do what it wants. The problem is that without control, the sea would <u>destroy</u> a lot of land by <u>floods</u> and <u>erosion</u>. Soft engineering approaches try to fit in with <u>natural</u> coastal processes to <u>protect habitats</u>.

- Beach nourishment — This simply means putting more mud or sand on the beach. The beach is an excellent natural flood defence, so by replacing all the sediment that's eroded, you can protect an area. The problem is how to get the sediment without causing <u>environmental damage</u> somewhere else. It's also pretty <u>expensive</u> and needs to be done again and again.

- Shoreline vegetation — Planting things like <u>marshbeds</u> on the shoreline <u>binds</u> the beach sediment together, slowing erosion. This also encourages shoreline <u>habitats</u> to develop.

- Dune stabilisation — Dunes are an excellent defence against <u>storms</u> and high tides. Sediment is added and erosion is <u>reduced</u> by footpath control. <u>Marram grass</u> can also be planted, which supports the dune ecosystem.

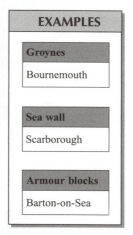
Dunes are good sea defences

- Set backs — Building houses set back from the coast.

- Managed retreat — This is about <u>slowing</u> coastal erosion but not trying to stop it. Eventually buildings will have to be moved or lost to the sea, but this can often be <u>cheaper</u> than investing in constant coastal control.

Section One
People & the Physical World

Case Study

In this section you'll need to demonstrate an understanding of the process of <u>coastal erosion</u> and the strategies used to limit it.
It's important that you use a real-life example so that you can show your understanding of how the theories work in real life.

Case Study: <u>Managing Coastal Erosion, Holderness, UK</u>

The <u>Holderness</u> coast lies between Flamborough Head and Spurn Head and is one of the fastest eroding coastlines in Europe. The average rate of erosion is 2 metres per year. Over 30 villages on the Holderness coast have fallen into the sea since Roman times.

There are lots of <u>erosional features</u> along the Holderness coast. The coastline is made up of soft clay and therefore experiences rapid <u>erosion</u>. In addition, <u>longshore drift</u> moves south along the coastline so there is little opportunity for beaches to become established in front of the cliffs.

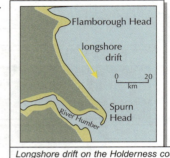

Longshore drift on the Holderness coast

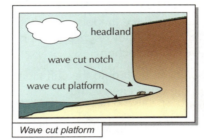

Wave cut platform

The erosional landforms evident along the coastline are varied. There is a <u>wave cut notch</u> and a <u>wave cut platform</u> at Flamborough Head. Flamborough Head is a <u>headland</u> and along the same coastline are <u>caves</u>, <u>arches</u> and <u>stacks</u>.

The towns and villages along this stretch of coast are constantly under threat from the encroaching sea. The coast needs to be <u>managed</u> to protect the settlements.

Hornsea

Hornsea is a town on the Holderness coastline that has nearly 3 km of shoreline fronting the town.

The coastline's position has been fixed artificially since the early 1900s, when <u>coastal defences</u> were erected.

A <u>concrete sea wall</u> protects the town from flooding. <u>Timber groynes</u> ensure that the sand and shingle beach is not washed away by longshore drift. These defences are regularly <u>repaired</u>.

South of Hornsea a <u>rock groyne</u> has been erected to protect a caravan park close to the shoreline.

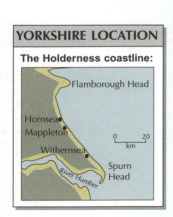

Mappleton

Mappleton is a village 3 km south of Hornsea. The village has been exposed to <u>rapid coastal erosion</u> at the rate of 2 metres per year.

In 1991, two <u>rock groynes</u> and a <u>rock revetment</u> were built. This meant that a beach accumulated between the groynes, providing a barrier against erosion.

Unfortunately the groynes are preventing sand from reaching the coastline to the south. This means that beyond the coastal defences <u>erosion</u> is continuing.

Revision Summary

Section One
People & the Physical World

Don't be put off by the size of this two-page revision summary. There's a lot to learn in this section, so it's broken down into different topics to make it easier for you to revise all the facts. Take a deep breath and work through the questions a section at a time. If there are any that you can't answer then go back and learn the facts some more. Keep doing this until you can answer all the questions — then you know you'll breeze the exam on this stuff.

> **EXAM TIP**
>
> Using words like 'tectonic', 'epicentre' and 'seismic' will show the examiner that you have a good scientific understanding of earthquakes and volcanoes.

Plate Tectonics, Earthquakes and Volcanoes

1) The Earth's crust is divided into plates. Name the places where they meet.
2) What causes the plates to move?
3) How quickly do plates move? Pick the right answer:
   a) a few metres per year,   b) a few millimetres per year.
4) What direction do the plates move in at a divergent margin?
5) Draw and label a plate margin with convergent plates. Explain what's happening.
6) What type of plate margin is caused by plates moving sideways against each other? Give an example.
7) Where is the main volcano zone in the world and what's it called?
8) Where do most earthquakes occur on the Earth's crust and why?
9) When studying earthquakes, what are:
   a) the focus,   b) the epicentre,   c) seismic waves?
10) How much bigger is a 6-point earthquake than a 5-point on the Richter scale?
11) How are volcanoes formed?
12) What are extinct, dormant and active volcanoes? Give one example of each.
13) What is a composite volcano made up of? Name an example.
14) Draw a composite volcano. Label the vent, crater, magma, ash and lava.
15) What are the pieces of rock that fly out of an erupting volcano called?
16) What is the difference between lava and magma?
17) Give four reasons why people live near volcanoes.
18) What do scientists look for to judge whether a volcano is about to erupt?
19) What do they look out for to predict earthquakes?
20) When did Mount St. Helens Erupt?
21) How did scientists know Mount St. Helens was going to erupt?
22) Where is Kobe? What happened there in 1995?
23) Where was the epicentre of the Kobe earthquake?
24) What are people doing to prevent another catastrophe in Kobe?

> **EXAM TIP**
>
> Doing practice questions is the only sure way of finding out what you know and what you don't know. So don't skip this page — it's important.

The Hydrological Cycle, Rivers and Floods

1) What is the input to the hydrological cycle?
2) Describe two ways that water can be stored in the hydrological cycle.
3) What is evapotranspiration?
4) Describe what the term drainage basin means.
5) What is a watershed?
6) What's the name of the place: a) where a river starts? b) where 2 rivers meet?
7) What is an estuary?
8) What happens to the long-profile of a river as you move downstream?
9) What is meant by lateral erosion, headward erosion, and vertical erosion?

Section One
People & the Physical World

Revision Summary

10) Name and describe the four ways a river transports its load.
11) When does a river deposit its load?
12) What are interlocking spurs? At which stage of a river are they found?
13) Draw diagrams to show how a waterfall is formed.
14) Draw a cross-section of a river meander. Add these labels: river cliff, point bar, strong current, weaker current, deep channel, shallow channel.
15) What is an ox-bow lake? How is it formed? Draw a diagram to show this.
16) Draw a storm hydrograph and add these labels: base flow, rising limb, falling limb, rainfall, lag time.
17) Name four factors which affect the tendency of a drainage basin to flood.
18) Explain the following terms:
    a) culverts, b) branching channels, c) relief channels.
19) Describe the disadvantages of hard engineering methods.
20) Describe five soft engineering methods of flood management.
21) Write a brief account to say why Bangladesh has horrendous floods. Include human and physical causes in your answer.
22) Name an example of a flood in an MEDC. What steps have been taken to avoid such problems in the future?
23) Explain why floods in LEDCs often cause bigger problems than floods in MEDCs.

EXAM TIP
Remember, hard engineering is increasingly being seen as a thing of the past, as it is expensive to maintain, and can be harmful to the environment.

Coastal Processes and Management

1) Explain the difference between constructive and destructive waves.
2) Name the five main types of coastal erosion. Write a brief description of each of them.
3) Describe with the aid of a diagram the term longshore drift.
4) Draw diagrams to show the formation of cliffs.
5) Describe how a wave cut platform is caused.
6) How does a headland and bay coastline form?
7) Describe how a crack in a headland can turn into a stack. Use diagrams to help you.
8) Name an example of: a) a series of stacks b) an arch.
9) Describe how the following are formed: a) beaches b) spits.
10) What is a tombolo? Give an example.
11) Describe the two ways that bars can form.
12) Name five hard engineering methods used to control coastal erosion. Explain how each one works.
13) Give four disadvantages of hard engineering techniques.
14) What is the difference between soft engineering and hard engineering? Which is more sustainable — soft engineering or hard engineering?
15) What is beach nourishment?
16) Why are sand dunes important in soft engineering?
17) What is meant by the term 'managed retreat'?
18) Name a settlement that is under threat from erosion on the Holderness coast.
19) How fast is the Holderness coast eroding?

EXAM TIP
Making a short list of all the key points for each case study is a good way to learn the facts that you need to know.

Population Distribution

**Section Two
People & Places to Live**

Population distribution is where people live —
this can be on a <u>global</u>, <u>regional</u> or <u>local</u> scale.

Population Distribution — *Where People Live*

Places with <u>lots</u> of people usually
have <u>habitable</u> environments.
They are either:

- <u>wealthy</u> and <u>industrial</u>
  e.g. Europe, Japan,
  eastern USA.

- <u>poor</u> with rapidly
  <u>growing</u> populations
  e.g. India, Kenya.

Places with <u>few</u> people are
usually <u>hostile environments</u>.

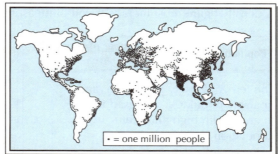

Map showing world population distribution

Large Populations Live in *Accessible Areas* with *Good Resources*

<u>River valleys</u> are <u>sheltered</u>. The river provides a <u>transport</u>
and <u>communication</u> link as well as a <u>water</u> supply.

<u>Lowland plains</u> are <u>flat</u> with <u>fertile soils</u> allowing productive
farming and easy <u>communication</u>.

Areas rich in <u>natural resources</u> can be important sources of materials for <u>industry</u>.
Resources include <u>fossil fuels</u> (coal, oil and gas) and <u>ores</u> like <u>iron</u> and <u>bauxite</u>.

<u>Coastal plains</u> often have <u>moderate</u> climates and good access
for international <u>trade</u> because they have sea <u>ports</u>.

EXAMPLES	
Areas of high population	
River Valleys	Ganges Valley (India), Rhine Valley (Germany)
Fertile lowland plains	East Anglia (cereals), Denmark (dairy farming)
Natural resources (coal)	South Wales coalfield, Ruhr Valley (Germany)
Coastal plains	New York

Accessibility of areas for population

Few People Live in Hostile Places *Without Resources*

<u>Areas with extreme climates</u> are almost empty. This is not only extremes of
temperature — lack of precipitation (<u>aridity</u>) is just as important.
Humans can cope with pretty hot and cold temperatures but we can't cope
without water. Even so, very hot and cold places such as Antarctica and the
Sahara Desert are good examples of places too extreme for people to live in.

<u>High altitudes</u> are <u>inaccessible</u>, have <u>poor soils</u> and <u>steep slopes</u> which
means that farming is difficult. This combination means that this
environment can support few people. A good example is the Andes
mountains in South America.

EXAMPLES	
Areas of low population	
Extreme climates	Antarctica, Sahara (N Africa)
High altitudes	Andes (S America), Himalayas (Asia), Atlas Mountains (Morocco)

Section Two
People & Places to Live

Population Density

We use population density and distribution to show the number of people living in different parts of the world.

FACT
Population density is influenced not only by physical factors (page 23), but also human factors such as politics, religious and cultural attitudes (see page 28), communications and labour force.

Population Density is a <u>Measurement</u> of <u>People</u> per km²

<u>Population density</u> is the average number of people living in an area. A density figure must include a unit of measurement — usually <u>per km²</u>.

$$\text{Population Density} = \frac{\text{Number of People}}{\text{Area}}$$

The terms '<u>densely populated</u>' and '<u>sparsely populated</u>' are used to refer to areas with high and low population densities.

<u>Population density</u> is an <u>average</u> number of people for the area and tells us <u>nothing</u> about where in that area people live. Example: in the diagrams the <u>density</u> of population is the same — 6 per km², but the <u>distribution</u> is different.

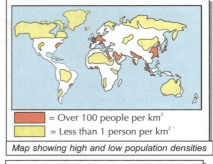

= Over 100 people per km²
= Less than 1 person per km²

Map showing high and low population densities

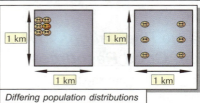

Differing population distributions

EXAMPLES
Population distribution in Asia

High density	**Singapore** 4608 people per km²
Low density	**Mongolia** 2 people per km²

EXAM TIP
Remember, opinions often vary on whether a country is overpopulated or not.

FACT
Overpopulation is a much more established and widespread problem than underpopulation. China has been trying to cope with its massive population for years. Underpopulation is rare — Switzerland and Germany now have very low birth rates and are starting to show signs of it.

Ideal Population Density Gives an <u>Optimum Population</u>

The concept of <u>optimum population</u> is about the ideal number of people that can be supported by the resources available. There are only <u>three terms</u> to learn:

<u>Overpopulation</u> — where there are <u>too many people</u> to be supported to a satisfactory level by the resources available.

Overpopulation

<u>Underpopulation</u> — where there are <u>too few people</u> to make the most of the resources available.

Underpopulation

<u>Optimum Population</u> — where the resources can be used to their <u>best advantage</u> without having too many people to maintain the standard of living.

You can Work Out <u>Regional Distribution</u> by Looking at <u>Densities</u>

By comparing the population densities of different areas, you get an idea of the population distribution over a larger area. This can be done on any scale — for the whole world, a continent, a country or smaller scale.

Population Structure

**Section Two
People & Places to Live**

Population structure is the number of males and females in different age groups. It's often shown as a pyramid with males and females on each side and the different ages making up the different sized layers.

Population *Pyramids* Show Population Structure

There are two basic population pyramid shapes.

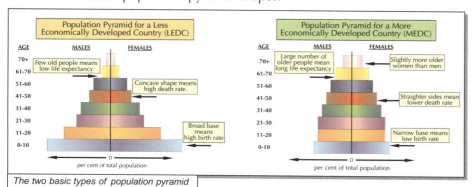

The two basic types of population pyramid

> **EXAM TIP**
>
> You need to be able to recognise the classic population pyramids for LEDCs and MEDCs — and interpret the causes and consequences of both.

There are 3 common variations on these basic shapes.

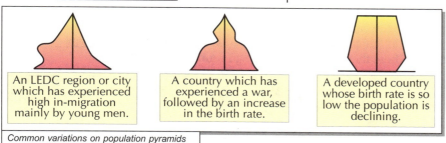

Common variations on population pyramids

> **SUMMARY**
>
> The structure of a population is determined by the proportion of males and females and the proportion of people in different age groups.

Demographic Terms are Used to Describe Populations

A high birth rate or death rate, or a steeply rising population indicates an LEDC. More children are born in LEDCs because less birth control is used. This is due to cultural and religious pressure, lack of contraception or lack of birth control education.

Infant Mortality rate — number of babies per thousand dying before they are one year old. A high infant mortality rate indicates an LEDC. This is because health care is worse in LEDCs.

Life Expectancy — the average number of years a person can expect to live. A high life expectancy indicates a good health care system and an MEDC.

Economically active — people between 16 and 64 years old (capable of earning a living). A high proportion of economically active people indicates high earning power — an MEDC.

Dependants — people of non-working age supported by the economically active. A high number of young dependants indicates a high birth rate and an LEDC. A high number of elderly dependants indicates a long life expectancy and an MEDC.

SUMMARY

Usual demographic features

	LEDCs	MEDCs
Birth rate	High	Low
Death rate	High	Low
Infant mortality rate	High	Low
Life Expectancy	Low	High
Proportion who are economically active	Low	High
Number of dependants	Many young	Many old

Section Two
People & Places to Live

Population Dependency in LEDCs & MEDCs

Population dependency is a ratio comparing the amount of people of working age (16 to 64) with the number of dependants — people aged under 16 or over 65.

EXAMPLE

The dependency ratio for the UK (1995 figures):

$$\frac{11{,}360{,}000 + 9{,}029{,}000}{37{,}867{,}000} \times 100$$

$$= \underline{53.84}$$

This means that, for every 100 economically active people, there are nearly 54 people who are not working.

Dependency is Measured Using the Dependency Ratio

It's normally written as a single number which is the number of dependants for every one hundred people of working age.
The dependency ratio is worked out using this formula:

$$\frac{\text{number of children (0-15) and old people (65+)}}{\text{number of people of working age (16–64)}} \times 100$$

High Dependency Levels can Cause Serious Problems

MEDCs usually have a dependency ratio of 50 – 70.
LEDCs can have one of over 100.

The higher the dependency ratio, the more stretched the country becomes, as wealth has to be more thinly spread. This puts added pressure on the country's workforce. This is a particular problem in LEDCs, where there is less wealth to go round in the first place.

The problems of a high dependency ratio

Young Dependants Put a Strain on LEDCs

High levels of education provision and health care are needed for children and babies. Most LEDCs cannot afford this. A population explosion is inevitable as these young people reach child bearing age.

The rapidly growing population need housing, and will need employment when they grow up. This is a serious concern for LEDCs.

EXAM TIP

Remember — on a global scale, high numbers of young dependants is typical of an LEDC, high numbers of elderly dependants is typical of an MEDC.

Elderly Dependants Put a Strain on MEDCs

High levels of health care are needed — and long term care of the elderly can be expensive. Facilities such as public transport and sheltered housing are required and must be planned for.

Unlike young dependants, elderly dependants are never going to enter the workforce, therefore they are an increasing and permanent financial strain on the shrinking number of economically active members of the population.

Population Change

**Section Two
People & Places to Live**

Population growth is a worrying matter. In some countries, the population is fairly stable, but in others, it's growing so fast that there's a strain on resources.

Population Growth is Affected by Three Factors

Birth rate — number of live babies born per thousand of the population per year.

Death rate — number of deaths per thousand of the population per year.

Migration — number of people moving in or out.
(Immigration is people moving into an area, emigration is people moving away.)

The World's Population is Growing Very Rapidly

The graph shows World Population Growth. It is not just the increase that's important — the rate of increase is getting faster.

The 20th Century has seen a population explosion. This means that a dramatic drop in the death rate has led to very rapid population growth.

The difference between the birth and death rates is the natural increase or natural decrease.

(It's 'increase' if the birth rate is higher and 'decrease' if the death rate is higher.)

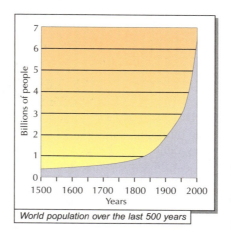

World population over the last 500 years

> **SUMMARY**
>
> Factors leading to population growth:
> - high birth rate
> - low death rate
> - high immigration
> - low emigration

Population Change Varies between Countries

Most countries experience population growth, but the rate of growth differs between different countries.

A high rate of growth happens when birth rates are high, but death rates are low.
A low rate of growth happens when both birth and death rates are low.

In many LEDCs, population growth is now very rapid — medical care has improved so the death rate has dropped, but the birth rate is still high.
In most MEDCs, population growth is now very slow.

> **FACT**
>
> A high rate of growth can be a problem for a country, as having too many people will put a strain on food supplies, raw materials, jobs and available land.

There are Reasons for Differing Birth Rates:

Reasons for high birth rates:
- No sex education or birth control (due to religious reasons, or lack of money).
- Parents have more children as some are expected to die.
- Children are needed to work and earn money to support the family.

Reasons for low birth rates:
- Birth control, sex education and abortions available, so unwanted babies can be avoided.
- Most children survive, so there's no need to have lots in case some die.
- Some people choose to have careers instead of families. Couples marry later to enjoy their freedom, have a career and earn money before having a family.

Section Two — People & Places to Live

Managing Population Growth

Population growth needs to be controlled, because the bigger the population, the greater the demand on resources.

Sustainable Development can Slow Population Increase

To avoid causing long-term damage to the planet, the population increase has to be slowed. LEDCs want to reduce the birth rate to slow population growth. To do this they need to break the vicious circle that causes the high birth rate.

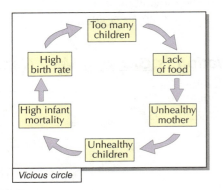
Vicious circle

EXAMPLES
Religious and cultural influences on population growth: • Pope John Paul II has continued the Roman Catholic Church's stance against contraception. • Islamic leaders are often opposed to birth control, and sometimes encourage the tradition of large families. • Chinese culture sometimes values boy babies more highly than girl babies.

The birth rate is influenced by cultural and religious customs which are very difficult to change. To combat these problems, many governments in LEDCs have encouraged family planning by educating women, opening clinics and providing contraception.

Population policies aim to increase the standard of living by reducing levels of malnutrition. This is linked with health policies.

Governments Play a Role in Controlling Population

Governments can either encourage or refuse immigration into their country.

On a local scale, planning and employment policies will affect decisions to move. For example, government grants are often given to companies to locate in deprived areas. This encourages people to move to the area for jobs, increasing the population, and improving the area's economy and status.

Migration Affects the Size of a Country's Population

Migration is the movement of people from one place to another (see pages 29 & 30 for more on migration).

International migration from LEDCs to MEDCs is usually economic migrants searching for a higher standard of living.

Some international migration is from MEDC to MEDC due to job opportunities or warmer climates. A brain drain is when highly qualified people move abroad for better opportunities.

Refugees are people who've been forced to leave their country due to war, hardship, natural disasters or political oppression. These can be large numbers or individuals.

EXAMPLES	
Types of migration	
Economic migrants	Mexico to wealthier USA
Climate	UK to warmer Australia
Brain drain	Scientists moving from UK to USA (better paid)
Refugees	Kosovans moving from Albania to UK in 1999 due to war

Refugees

Migration

Section Two — People & Places to Live

International migration from LEDCs to MEDCs is usually economic migrants searching for a higher standard of living.

There are Three Types of Migration

International Migration — when people move from one country to another. This can be across the world, or just a few miles over a border.

Regional Migration — moving to another region in the same country.

Local Migration — when people move a short distance within the same region.

TIP: See page 28 for more details on the reasons for migration.

Migration can be Classified by Reason

Migration happens because of push and pull factors. Learn the two boxes below to make sure you know the difference. Remember — it's usually a combination of the two that causes migration.

Push factors

These are the things about the origin that make someone decide to move. They are usually negative things such as lack of job or education opportunities.

Pull factors

These are things about the destination that attract people. They are usually positive things such as job opportunities or the perception of a better standard of living.

Governments Play an Important Role in Migration

Governments can either encourage or refuse immigration into their country through their policies. On a local scale, planning and employment policies will affect decisions to move (see page 28 for more on this).

EXAMPLE: Countries' policies for accepting immigrants vary considerably. For example, Britain's immigration policies are fairly relaxed compared with other European countries, like Germany.

Be Clear about the Right Terms:

The words used to describe migration all sound pretty similar, so make sure you learn the difference between them really well.

EMIGRANT — Someone moving OUT of a country. (ORIGIN)

MIGRANT — A person moving from one area to another.

IMMIGRANT — Someone moving INTO a country. (DESTINATION)

Important terms used to describe migration

Section Two
People & Places to Live

Case Studies

You need to know case studies about how population can be managed, and the causes and consequences of such management.

Case Study 1: Population Management — China

25% of the world's population is Chinese. In 1979, the government introduced a 'one child policy' to control population growth.

The policy:
Couples had to gain permission from family planning officials for each birth. Birth control was strictly enforced. People who had unauthorised children were given big fines. Authorised children were given benefits such as free education, health care, pensions and family benefits — unauthorised children were given no benefits, schooling or employment opportunities.

In 1982, couples with more than two children were forced to be sterilised (mainly women). Unauthorised pregnancies were often terminated by forced abortion.

WORLD LOCATION

ASIAN LOCATION

Effects of the policy:
The policy resulted in a high rate of infanticide (killing newborn children). 90% of foetuses aborted in China are female because Chinese tradition values boys above girls. Because of this, China now has many more boys than girls — it has created an 'army of bachelors'.

Recently the government has used less extreme methods (e.g. birth control education) with good results. It is estimated that without the policy there would be an extra 320 million people in China.

Modern Chinese family

Case Study 2: Migration from Turkey to Germany

Since World War II, a large number of Turks have migrated to Germany, increasing Germany's population.

Reasons for migrating:
Many Turks felt they had to leave their homeland because there was limited industry and employment was hard to find (push factors).

Turks were also attracted to Germany because they expected a better life including good jobs, better pay, good health care, etc (pull factors).

Germany was in a very bad condition after World War II and there was a great demand for help rebuilding the country. Turks were welcomed into the country.

EUROPEAN LOCATION

Problems caused by migration:
When the German economy began to slow down there were fewer employment opportunities. Unemployment began to rise and many Turkish immigrants found themselves out of work.

Many Turks found it hard to learn German, which led to the two groups becoming isolated from each other. After the reunification of East and West Germany in 1989, East Germans began to work for low pay in the former West Germany, causing conflict with the Turks. Competition for employment between Turks and Germans led to further racial unrest.

Urbanisation

**Section Two
People & Places to Live**

Urbanisation occurs in both MEDCs and LEDCs.
It can create various problems in both rural and urban areas.

The Definition of Urbanisation

Urbanisation is the process by which an increasing proportion of the population become town or city dwellers. The important word is proportion — urbanisation is only occurring if the growth rate of cities is greater than the growth rate of the whole population. Urbanisation is happening on a global scale.
It's also happening on a regional scale in LEDCs.

There are Three Causes of Urbanisation in LEDCs

- Rural-urban migration is occurring on a massive scale due to population pressure and lack of resources in rural areas. People from rural areas often believe that the standard of living is higher in cities (even though this often turns out not to be the case).

- The infrastructure of cities in LEDCs is expanding faster than in the rural areas, which attracts industrial investment and people looking for work.

- Population increase tends to be faster in urban areas because health care facilities are better, so the death rate is lower. Also, the people moving to cities are younger and so have more children.

EXAMPLES

The figures below show the estimated rank order of the world's largest cities for 2010.

Rank	City
1	Tokyo
2	Mumbai
3	Shanghai
4	Lagos
5	São Paulo
6	Jakarta
7	Mexico City
8	Beijing
9	Karachi
10	New York

In 1970, this list would have contained such cities as London, Los Angeles, Paris and Moscow. Now the largest cities are mainly in LEDCs.

Urbanisation has Created Millionaire Cities

Millionaire cities are cities with over a million inhabitants. The world's largest city is Tokyo with an estimated population of 28.7 million for the year 2010. (That's the same as half the total UK population.) The only other MEDC city in the top 10 ranking is New York, which has a population of around 17 million.

Aerial view of New York City

Urbanisation Affects Rural and Urban Areas of a Country

It's not just the urban areas that are affected by urbanisation — the nature of rural areas changes too.

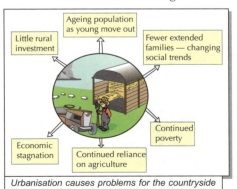
Urbanisation causes problems for the countryside

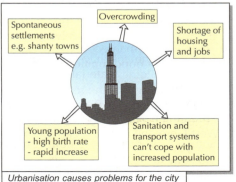
Urbanisation causes problems for the city

**Section Two
People & Places to Live**

Urban Problems in LEDCs

Urban areas of LEDCs have a number of problems.

Spontaneous Settlements are Common to LEDC Cities

Spontaneous settlements, or shanty towns, are a problem in many LEDC cities. They are settlements built illegally by the very poor, because the city can't provide enough housing for all it's people, many of whom can't afford proper housing. Most of the inhabitants are rural-urban migrants. The settlements are badly built, without basic amenities. However, through time, the inhabitants may manage to improve their shanty town.

Shanty town

FACT
Spontaneous settlements are also known as shanty towns or squatter settlements. Many countries have their own names for them though, e.g. favelas in Brazil, and bustees in India.

EXAMPLES

Cities with shanty towns
São Paulo, Brazil
Calcutta, India

Overcrowding is a Major Problem in *LEDC* Cities

Competition for land is intense. High populations and lack of available transport mean people want to live near places where they might find work.

Overcrowding puts pressure on services such as sanitation, health care and housing provision. LEDCs can rarely afford to provide these services for everyone. This leads to problems with clean water supply and waste disposal, which can create major health risks.

The limited land available means that shanty towns are often built on dangerous ground such as steep hillsides which may collapse in heavy rain, or on rubbish tips (a source of livelihood for some). Overcrowding makes the problem worse.

Rural-Urban Migration Makes Urban Problems Worse

The rapid rate of migration means it's impossible to know exactly how fast the cities are growing — population numbers are only estimates. This makes planning for growth very difficult.

While LEDCs have huge debts there is little chance of the urban problems being solved, as they cannot afford the resources they need to sort things out.

EXAMPLE
São Paulo in Brazil and New Delhi in India are places whose squatter settlements have benefited from self-help schemes.

Rohini in New Delhi is a community which was built in the 1980s to house people from old squatter settlements.

Squatter Settlements can be *Improved*

Some governments have tried to remove squatter settlements by simply destroying them. This rarely works as the settlements soon reappear.

Some governments have introduced self-help schemes, where they provide building materials for the residents of squatter settlements on the understanding that the residents carry out the building work themselves. However, money is short and the schemes are often inadequate for the large numbers involved.

Some governments have built completely new communities away from the old squatter settlements. The new settlements have good links to the CBD, which means employment is easier to find.

Urban Land Use in MEDCs

**Section Two
People & Places to Live**

Land use is exactly what you'd expect it to be —
what land is used for, like for housing or factories.

Land Use Models Describe Patterns in Cities

Two models of land use that apply to MEDCs are the concentric zone model (devised by Burgess) and the sector model (devised by Hoyt).

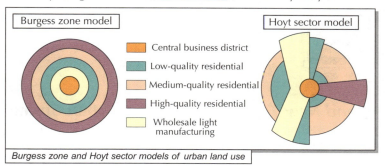
Burgess zone and Hoyt sector models of urban land use

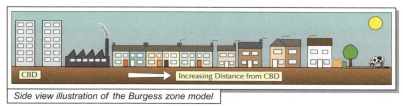
Side view illustration of the Burgess zone model

> **EXAM TIP**
>
> These models are generalisations, to give you an idea of how land use is roughly organised. It doesn't mean that all cities will follow the same pattern, and you shouldn't expect them to. All cities have their own little quirks and differences.

The concentric zone model, or Burgess zone model, says that the centre is the oldest part of the city and building spreads out from the middle. This means the newest parts of the city will be on the edge — the outer suburbs.

The Hoyt sector model expands this idea to take into account industrial development along the main routeways into and out of a city.

Models have *Functional Zones* showing *Land Use*

The Central Business District (CBD) is the commercial centre of the city. It contains shops and offices, transport routes meet here and it has high land values as there is intense competition for space. Buildings are usually tall and building density is very high. Very few people live in the CBD.

The zone of transition or inner city is the area of wholesale manufacturing. It is a mix of poorer quality housing and old industrial buildings which are often run down, as well as newer housing and light industrial development where derelict land has been cleared. Sometimes these areas have been redeveloped and they can become desirable places to live.

The housing areas are older near the CBD where old terraced housing remains. There are newer housing estates toward the edge of the city and more expensive housing on the outskirts, where land is cheaper and houses and gardens can be bigger. Dormitory villages on the edge of cities house people who like to live in the country and work in the city.

It's important to remember these models are generalisations and real places are all different. In recent years, out-of-town shopping centres and the replacement of inner city tower blocks with housing estates on the urban fringe has begun to change land use patterns. New housing is now often built on brownfield sites (cleared derelict land) instead of the settlement's edges.

> **KEY TERM**
>
> Gentrification is the term given to the process of improving inner city areas by renovating old, existing buildings and making them desirable places to live.

> **EXAMPLE**
>
> Gentrification has featured a lot in Glasgow, where many of the traditionally working-class tenement flats have been converted into desirable, expensive housing.

Section Two
People & Places to Live

Planning and the Rural-Urban Fringe

Planning prevents the countryside being eaten up by new buildings. This is called <u>checking urban sprawl</u>, and usually happens at the <u>rural-urban fringe</u> — where the city and the country meet.

Urban Sprawl leads to Growth of <u>Conurbations</u>

A conurbation's urban sprawl

<u>Urban sprawl</u> occurs when the <u>outward growth</u> of cities is left <u>unchecked</u>, and the city gradually takes up more and more of the surrounding countryside. A <u>conurbation</u> is formed when one city grows so large that it <u>encompasses</u> surrounding towns, forming one huge urban area.

> **EXAMPLE**
> An example of a conurbation in the UK is the West Midlands Conurbation, where Birmingham has expanded to merge with Wolverhampton, Dudley, Solihull, West Bromwich, Walsall and Sutton Coldfield.

<u>Greenbelts</u> and <u>New Towns</u> — Checking Urban Sprawl

<u>Greenbelts</u> are areas around cities designed to stop urban sprawl. They were set up around most of the UK's large cities in the 1940s, and building is restricted within them. However, some greenbelts have now been released for <u>development</u> due to the need for new housing.

Limiting urban sprawl meant there was a shortage of housing space in the cities, so <u>new towns</u> were built beyond the greenbelt to house the <u>overspill population</u>. This policy has been used in many countries, including LEDCs.

> **EXAMPLE**
> Greenbelts don't always work — e.g. the M25 motorway was built on London's greenbelt, and several hundred hectares of Newcastle's greenbelt were released for new housing.

The <u>Rural-Urban Fringe</u> Needs Planning for <u>Leisure</u>

<u>Leisure amenities</u> for urban dwellers are found on the rural-urban fringe because they are easily accessible here, and need more space than can be found in cities.

Amenities such as <u>golf courses</u>, <u>country parks</u> and <u>riding stables</u> have grown in recent years as increased car ownership has meant more people have access to the countryside. <u>Farmers</u> have found that they can make money by expanding into leisure activities such as '<u>pick your own</u>' fruit centres or <u>rare breeds</u> visitor centres which provide a family day out. These facilities have changed the character of the rural-urban fringe.

> **EXAMPLE**
> The most famous example of a new town is Milton Keynes, but there are over 30 new towns in the UK.

Planning has to get Clever when there's <u>No Room Left</u>

<u>More people</u> means there's a need for <u>more houses</u>.

- <u>Osaka, Japan</u> — Osaka is a very packed (10 000 people per km^2), growing city with tiny houses. When all the flat land was inhabited, houses were built over the sea — this is called <u>land reclamation</u>. The new island provided more <u>spacious</u> housing with facilities and good transport links, <u>easing pressure</u> on Osaka city.

Reclaimed land in Osaka

- <u>São Paulo, Brazil</u> — Many poor people who move to the city for work end up living in favelas (shanty towns). A new <u>self-help housing scheme</u> is providing low-cost improvements. <u>Local people</u> do the work, and the <u>government</u> provides materials, electricity and sewage pipes.

- <u>Liverpool, UK</u> — An increasing <u>demand</u> for housing and government incentives for using <u>brownfield</u> sites has led to the <u>dockside redevelopment</u>, which provides housing and shops in a previously run-down area.

Liverpool dockland redevelopment

Improving the Urban Environment

Section Two
People & Places to Live

Urban areas in MEDCs experience a number of problems including inadequate housing, traffic congestion and general decline, all of which must be reduced.

Housing can be *Improved*

In the 1960s, the lack of space in the inner cities led to the construction of high-rise tower blocks to replace inadequate housing.

In many cases, tower blocks created new problems. The standard of living was poor, overcrowding was still a problem and the lack of community spirit led to increased crime.

In the 1980s, the British government introduced a policy of urban renewal, or gentrification. This meant existing buildings would be improved rather than completely replaced. This strategy is now a common practice in many British cities.

Traffic needs to be *Managed*

Traffic congestion is a serious problem in most cities, but especially in those in MEDCs where there can be more vehicles.

One solution to the problems of traffic congestion is to improve and extend public transport to encourage people to use private cars less. For example, bus systems can be improved, or new tram systems introduced. Reducing traffic makes cities more sustainable because they cause less pollution, and it improves the quality of life for the people who use the cities.

Many cities have introduced park and ride schemes that reduce the amount of traffic entering the city centre.

Some cities have restricted vehicle access to the city centre through the pedestrianisation of certain areas.

Many cities have reduced the amount of traffic travelling through the city centre by building ring roads around the city.

Pedestrianisation in a city centre

EXAMPLES	
Types of traffic management in the UK:	
Tram systems	Manchester, Sheffield
Park and ride schemes	Oxford, Nottingham
Pedestrianisation	Oxford, York
Ring roads	Watford, Leicester

Urban Regeneration is about *Improving Inner Cities*

Many inner city areas have suffered from high crime rates, vandalism and unemployment. Urban regeneration is an attempt to renew and improve these areas. There are a number of strategies involved in urban regeneration:

- Improved public transport and access to areas encourages people to live and work in inner city areas, like the London docklands.
- Low tax rates and rents are used to attract large businesses and reduce unemployment.
- Community centres and services have been introduced to areas to improve the quality of life.
- Many cities have spent money on the gentrification of buildings to improve their appearance and make them more attractive to people.

London docklands redevelopment

EXAMPLES	
Types of urban regeneration:	
Improved public transport	Manchester, London docklands
Low tax rates and rent	Salford Quays in Manchester
Community centres and services	Sheffield, Leeds
Gentrification of buildings	Newcastle, Cardiff

Section Two — People & Places to Live

The Settlement Hierarchy

A <u>settlement</u> is where people live, and a <u>hierarchy</u> is a system of ranking things. A <u>settlement hierarchy</u> is therefore a rank order of settlements.

Settlements are Ranked by <u>Population Size</u>

As settlement size <u>increases</u>, the number <u>decreases</u> — so there are many villages, but few conurbations. The diagram below shows the general pattern.

EXAMPLES	
Conurbation	Birmingham
City	Lincoln
Large town	Doncaster, South Yorkshire
Small town	Gainsborough, Lincolnshire
Village	Heapham, Lincolnshire

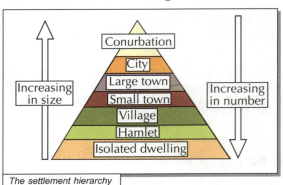

The settlement hierarchy

Be <u>careful</u> — there are examples of cities which are smaller than towns. The <u>number of services</u> provided in a settlement <u>increases</u> with settlement size. Large places provide high and low order goods and services. Small ones provide only low order goods and services.

A Settlement's Size indicates its <u>Sphere of Influence</u>

The terms <u>sphere of influence</u>, <u>urban field</u>, <u>catchment area</u>, <u>market area</u> and <u>hinterland</u> all mean the same thing. It is <u>the area served</u> by the goods, services, administration and employment provided by a settlement (or central place) and which provides <u>agricultural produce</u> and <u>leisure facilities</u> (such as country parks, golf courses etc.) for the settlement.

<u>Small central places have small hinterlands</u> because the goods and services they provide are low order (i.e. everyday stuff like bread, milk and newspapers). <u>Large central places have large hinterlands</u> because they provide a wide variety of high order goods and services (such as specialist shops, a large hospital) as well as low order goods and services, and people will travel further to use them. This leads to something called <u>central place theory</u>.

<u>Central place theory</u> states that <u>large towns</u> encompass their own hinterland, plus the smaller hinterlands of surrounding <u>smaller towns</u>, which in turn encompass the hinterlands of surrounding <u>villages</u>.

EXAMPLES
Large out-of-town shopping centres include Meadowhall near Sheffield and the Metro Centre near Gateshead.

Out-of-Town Shopping Centres are a New Development

Recently, many regional shopping centres have been developed around the UK. Most of these regional shopping centres are situated in <u>out-of-town</u> locations. The centres are popular with developers and shoppers for a number of reasons:

- The land they occupy was cheap to buy.
- They are situated in or near to areas with a high population.
- They are accessible by car and train, with little traffic congestion and good parking facilities.
- There are shopping and leisure facilities in the same place.

Due to declining population and competition from large supermarkets, village shops are struggling to survive. In most villages it is unusual to find many shops.

Counter-Urbanisation

Section Two
People & Places to Live

Counter-urbanisation is the movement <u>out of cities</u> to the surrounding more rural areas. It has recently been happening in many MEDCs.

There are <u>Six Reasons</u> for <u>Counter-Urbanisation</u>

- <u>Growth in transport</u> and <u>communications</u> mean people no longer have to live where they work. Motorways and increased car ownership have led to <u>commuting</u>. The growth of <u>information technology</u> — faxes, e-mail and video conferencing — means more people can work from home.
- <u>Government policies</u> can encourage movement out of cities, e.g. setting up <u>fast transport links</u> to '<u>satellite</u>' towns and villages.
- <u>New business parks</u> on out-of-town greenfield sites mean people no longer have to travel to city centres to work and prefer to live on the outskirts of cities to be nearer their work.
- <u>Pollution</u> and <u>traffic congestion</u> in cities encourage people to live in rural areas.
- More people have the <u>money</u> to own <u>second homes</u> in the countryside or <u>move house</u> when they <u>retire</u>.
- <u>House prices</u> in cities have become very high — people are moving out to find cheaper housing.

> **EXAMPLE**
>
> Many of the employees at the large greenfield Cambridge science park live outside Cambridge, in smaller towns like Huntingdon and Ely.

Counter-Urbanisation has a <u>Dramatic Effect</u> on <u>Villages</u>

Village <u>character</u> and <u>function</u> have changed due to the influx of people who work in urban areas. Learn this flow diagram which shows you how.

> **EXAMPLE**
>
> Thurston, near Bury-St-Edmonds in Suffolk, was once a small agricultural village. Now it is home to lots of people who commute to work in London. The rural nature of the village has disappeared, as have the local village shops. House prices have also increased so they're higher than most local people can afford.

- <u>Movement into village</u> of people working in urban areas who want to live in the country.
  ⇩
- A more <u>affluent population</u> and higher <u>car ownership</u> mean people use services in the city, <u>not</u> local services.
  ⇩
- An increase in <u>house prices</u> means young people <u>can't afford</u> homes and move away.
  ⇩
- The village is largely <u>empty</u> during the <u>day</u> — called a <u>dormitory village</u>. This leads to a decline in the community spirit.
  ⇩
- Local shops and services <u>close down</u> as few people use them. Rural transport provision is also <u>reduced</u> as it is non-economic.
  ⇩
- Local people without transport have <u>access</u> to fewer <u>amenities</u> — the young and old become <u>isolated</u>.

Quiet dormitory village

Section Two — People & Places to Live

Case Studies

It's important that you can show you understand <u>urban planning</u> by referring to case studies.

Case Study 1: <u>Urban Traffic Management in Glasgow</u>

In the past, Glasgow has experienced a number of problems caused by traffic in the <u>city centre</u>, such as pollution, congestion and road accidents. Glasgow City Council has tried to <u>tackle</u> these problems in a number of ways:

UK LOCATION

- <u>Parking charges</u> have been introduced in the city centre to discourage people from driving into the city.

- The city's <u>bus service</u> has been improved to encourage more people to use buses instead of private cars. <u>Bus priority lanes</u> have been introduced to prevent buses getting stuck in traffic congestion.

- People are being encouraged to cycle into and around the city. <u>Cycle lanes</u> are being constructed all around the city and cycle parking areas have been provided.

- <u>Rail travel</u> has been improved and the services are becoming more popular with the public.

- The <u>underground rail system</u> has been improved with new trains and a <u>park and ride</u> scheme, which encourages people to leave their cars outside the city centre and travel in on the underground.

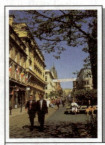
Cleaner, safer Glasgow

Case Study 2: <u>Urban Regeneration in Nottingham</u>

There were a number of <u>run-down areas</u> in Nottingham's CBD, such as Lenton, Radford and St. Ann's. These areas suffered from old housing, poor facilities, run-down schools and high crime rates. From the 1970s onwards, there has been an <u>urban redevelopment programme</u> to try and improve these areas:

UK LOCATION

- <u>Grants</u> have been made available to refurbish buildings.

- New <u>houses</u> with modern facilities have been built.

- New <u>schools</u> have been built and <u>workshops</u> set up to create employment.

- Open spaces have been created to provide <u>recreation facilities</u> like sports grounds.

- Derelict land has been cleared to improve the appearance of the area.

- <u>Traffic calming measures</u> have been introduced to make the roads safer for pedestrians.

- Some <u>industrial areas</u> have been converted into housing and the industries have been moved to suburban areas.

Radford Mill, Nottingham, turned into offices

Case Studies

Section Two
People & Places to Live

You also need to know case studies of <u>urban land use</u> in an MEDC and an LEDC. The case studies on this page show land use in <u>Paris</u>, France (an MEDC), and in a <u>squatter settlement</u> in <u>New Delhi</u>, India (an LEDC).

Case Study 1: <u>Urban Land Use in Paris, France</u>

Paris has four distinct zones which differ in terms of their land use:

Central Business District (CBD):
- Banking, commercial and shopping areas.
- Some exclusive, high-quality housing.
- Many <u>culturally important</u> buildings such as Notre Dame Cathedral, Pompidou Exhibition Centre and the Louvre art gallery.

The Louvre in Paris's CBD

Inner zones:
- Some small <u>industries</u> still operate (e.g. the Dior and Chanel fashion houses).
- Some <u>redeveloped housing</u> and smaller <u>shopping</u> zones.

Outer suburbs:
- The population of areas like Versailles and St. Denis is rising because there is very little <u>housing</u> in the inner city.
- There are a number of <u>shopping centres</u> to serve the growing population (e.g. St. Denis).
- There are numerous open-air <u>recreation</u> areas (e.g. the Bois de Boulogne).

Open-air recreation area in Paris

Rural-urban fringe:
- <u>Heavy industries</u> make bulky products on the north-eastern fringe.
- Modern <u>electronic industries</u> are mainly located in the outer suburbs.
- Five new <u>satellite towns</u> have been developed on the fringes to accommodate Paris's growing population.

Case Study 2: <u>Squatter Settlements in New Delhi, India</u>

People are drawn to New Delhi from rural areas because life in the countryside is hard (<u>push factor</u>). They believe that they will find jobs and a better standard of living in the city (<u>pull factor</u>). However, many of these people end up living in <u>jhuggies</u> (squatter settlements) which are found on the urban fringe by roads and in dangerous areas.

There are 400 000 shanty homes housing over 2.4 million people. They have a very high <u>population density</u> and very <u>poor facilities</u>. These terrible conditions have led to a high rate of <u>disease</u> including cholera and dysentery. The people hope that the government will provide <u>services</u> like electricity and sewerage.

Rather than destroying the jhuggies, the New Delhi authorities are using them as a starting point for <u>urban redevelopment</u>.

The government are providing the <u>materials</u> for rebuilding while the residents themselves are <u>developing</u> the buildings. They have also built completely <u>new settlements</u> with good transport links to the CBD.

Section Two
People & Places to Live

Revision Summary

It's the end of a huge section all about people and places to live. You've done well to get this far, but it's not quite over yet. Go through the questions below, answering them as best you can. Then go back, check your answers, correct them and repeat the whole process until you can do them all.

Population

1) Which parts of the world have very few people? Give some examples.
2) Which parts of the world have lots of people? Explain why and give examples.
3) Give two reasons why river valleys are densely populated.
4) Define the term 'population density'. How does it differ from 'distribution'?
5) Define 'overpopulation', 'underpopulation' and 'optimum population'.
6) Draw and label the typical population pyramids for an LEDC and an MEDC.
7) Make a list of the population characteristics that can be identified in a population pyramid.
8) Draw and label a population pyramid shape for each of the following:
    a) An LEDC city or region which has experienced high in-migration by young men.
    b) A country that has experienced war and then an increase in the birth rate.
    c) A developed country with a low birth rate and a declining population.
9) Explain what 'infant mortality rate' means.
10) Do the following terms describe an LEDC or an MEDC?
    a) high life expectancy   b) high number of elderly dependants
    c) high number of young dependants   d) high infant mortality rate
11) Write down the formula for working out the dependency ratio.
12) Give three problems for countries with a high number of young dependants.
13) Give three problems for a country with an increasingly ageing population.
14) Define the following terms: birth rate, death rate, natural increase.
15) Sketch a graph of the world's population over the last 500 years.
16) What is a 'population explosion'? What causes it?
17) Explain what 'natural increase' and 'natural decrease' mean.
18) Give three reasons for birth rates being high.
19) Does the trend for concentrating on a career lead to high or low birth rates?
20) Draw the diagram showing the link between high birth rates and health. Why is the health of women in LEDCs so important?
21) Describe how migration can affect a country's population.
22) Describe China's policy for reducing the population. Include: its name, the year it was brought in, how it's enforced, the name for killing newborn children and the effect on the population pyramid.
23) Why did Turks migrate to Germany and what problems did it cause?

EXAM TIP

We've said it before and we'll say it again — doing practice questions is the only sure way of finding out what you know and what you don't know. So don't skip this page — it's important.

Revision Summary

Section Two
People & Places to Live

Settlement

1) In terms of migration, define the terms 'push factors' and 'pull factors'.
2) Define these terms: immigrant, migrant, emigrant.
3) What is the definition of urbanisation?
4) What are the three causes of urbanisation in LEDCs?
5) What are millionaire cities? Name two examples — one from an MEDC and one from an LEDC.
6) List the problems of urbanisation in the countryside (give six) and the city (give five).
7) Give two other names for shanty towns.
8) Describe two negative consequences of overcrowding in LEDC cities.
9) How can squatter settlements be improved?
10) Draw the diagrams to show the concentric zone model and the sector model of urban land use.
11) Define these terms: CBD, zone of transition, gentrification, dormitory village, brownfield site.
12) What is a conurbation?
13) Explain why greenbelts and new towns were necessary.
14) What is the rural-urban fringe, and what are its characteristics?
15) Describe the planning initiatives in Osaka, São Paulo and Liverpool.
16) What strategies are being adopted to solve the problem of traffic congestion in MEDC cities?
17) List four strategies involved in urban regeneration.
18) Draw the diagram to show the settlement hierarchy (there are seven bits).
19) What is an area's sphere of influence?
20) Give examples of high and low order goods.
21) Why are hinterlands usually shown as hexagons in diagrams?
22) Why are out-of-town shopping centres popular with developers?
23) Give two reasons why shoppers like out-of-town shopping centres.
24) What is counter-urbanisation? Is it happening mainly in MEDCs or LEDCs?
25) Give six reasons for counter-urbanisation.
26) Describe the six-stage process by which counter-urbanisation changes the character of villages.
27) List the ways in which Glasgow has tried to manage its traffic problem.
28) Describe the urban regeneration which has taken place in Nottingham.
29) How do the four zones of Paris differ in terms of their land use?
30) What are the problems found in New Delhi's squatter settlements? How is the government trying to solve these problems?

> **EXAM TIP**
> Look at a good road map, or an OS map, if you have one. Try to identify places you think might be new towns. What makes you think they're new towns?

> **EXAM TIP**
> Look on a map for possible green belt areas. Then see if you can work out which bits of a town or city are used for which type of land use. How does it compare to the Burgess zone model?

Section Three
People and their Needs

Contrasts in Development

Developed and developing countries have different characteristics around the world.

The World's Wealth is Not Shared Out Equally

The world can be divided into richer and poorer countries.

Wealthier countries are known as More Economically Developed Countries, or MEDCs.

Poorer countries are described as Less Economically Developed Countries, or LEDCs. They're also called developing countries or the third world. This term came from a time when MEDCs were known as the 'first world', the former communist countries were the 'second world', and the rest were the 'third world'.

MEDC city

25% of the world's population live in MEDCs and own 80% of the world's wealth.

The term development refers to how mature a country's economy, infrastructure and social systems are — the more developed a country's economic systems are, the wealthier it is.

The 'development gap' is the contrast between rich and poor countries. It's best shown by comparing the estimated GNP per capita of a rich and a poor country (see page 43).

LEDC village

> **EXAMPLE**
> An example of the development gap:
> In 1995, the estimated GNP per capita of Switzerland was $40,630. For Tanzania it was $140.

The North-South Divide Separates Developed and Developing Countries

The map of rich and poor countries can be split by a line called the north-south divide.

The richer countries are almost all in the northern hemisphere — except Australia and New Zealand. Poorer countries are mostly in the tropics and the southern hemisphere.

The north-south divide, as defined in the Brandt Report (1979)

Places that suffer natural disasters like droughts are often developing countries.

The richer countries mainly have temperate (moderate) climates and good natural resources (although there are exceptions, like Japan). This meant these countries developed their industry first and became dominant in the world economy.

The explanations for the north-south divide have as much to do with political history as they do with physical geography. Many MEDCs had colonies in LEDCs and there are still restrictions imposed on world trade — this means the development gap is getting wider.

> **SUMMARY**
> Don't forget the exceptions in the north-south divide: Australia and New Zealand are in the southern hemisphere, but are MEDCs, and Japan is an MEDC but has few natural resources.

Measuring Development

Section Three
People and their Needs

The concept of LEDCs and MEDCs is fairly straightforward, but measuring a country's development is more tricky — because there are so many indicators of development. (NB. Indicators are sometimes called indices.)

Development Indices — Comparing Development Levels

The following indicators can be used to measure development:

1) Gross Domestic Product (GDP): Total value of goods and services produced in a year for the total population. Gross National Product (GNP) is similar but includes invisible earnings like foreign investments. This is useful but says nothing about distribution of wealth — so it can be misleading. GNP or GDP per capita are therefore more useful — they reveal the total value of goods and services produced in a year per person.

2) Life expectancy: Average age a person can expect to live to — this is higher for women.

3) Infant mortality rate: Number of babies who die under 1 year old, per thousand live births.

4) Calorie intake: Average number of calories eaten per day — at least 2500 are needed for an adult to stay healthy.

5) Energy consumption: Weight of coal (or equivalent) used per person per year — an indication of levels of industry.

6) Urban population: Percentage of the total population living in towns and cities.

7) Literacy rates: Percentage of adults who can read well enough to get by.

8) Health service provision: Things like the number of patients per doctor.

	UK	ETHIOPIA
1 GNP per capita	$28,700	$100
2	women 77 yrs, men 74 yrs	women 48 yrs, men 46 yrs
3	6 per thousand	120 per thousand
4	3,317 per day	1,610 per day
5	54 tonnes	0.03 tonnes
6	80%	15%
7	99%	36%
8	300	32,500

Comparison of development indices for the UK and Ethiopia

EXAM TIP
It's really important that you know the precise definitions of all these development indices. Make sure you can say how each should look for a rich and a poor country, and learn the problems of using them to measure development too.

EXAMPLE
People in LEDCs have a poorer variety, quality and amount of food available. There are often famines as the food supply is unreliable. For example, in the poorest regions of Nepal, people depend on farming for food, but the physical conditions for farming are bad. Improvements have been made through the introduction of new high-yield varieties of crops, and new breeds of cattle and sheep. A new milk marketing scheme now helps farmers supply milk to urban areas, creating extra income.

Many of these indices are linked, and relationships can be identified — for example countries with high GDP tend to have high urban populations and consume a lot of energy. These relationships can also be used to identify a country's level of development.

There are Two Main Problems with the Indices

Some countries may appear to be developed according to some indices but not others — as a country develops, some aspects develop before others. No measurement should be used on its own — it should be balanced with other indices to avoid any inaccuracies.

Up-to-date information isn't always available — maybe because a country doesn't have the administration necessary to compile and publish it, or because they don't want the information to be available publicly. This can make comparisons between countries difficult.

Section Three
People and their Needs

Classification of Industry

There are four types of industry. They are classified according to their processes.

Primary Industry Involves Collecting Raw Materials

Raw materials are anything naturally present in or on the earth before processing. They are collected in three ways:
- They can be quarried, mined or drilled for below the Earth's surface — coal mining and oil drilling are primary industries.
- They can be grown — e.g. farming and forestry.
- They can be collected from the sea — e.g. fishing.

Primary industry

EXAMPLES
Types of industry:

Primary	Farmer grows potatoes
Secondary	Factory processes potatoes into crisps
Tertiary	Shopkeeper sells crisps
Quaternary	Scientists research new production methods

Secondary Industry is Manufacturing a Product

A secondary industry is where a product from primary industry is turned into another product. The finished product of one secondary industry may be raw material for another, e.g. one factory may make tyres which are then sent on to be used in another secondary industry, e.g. a factory that makes cars.

Tertiary Industry Provides a Service

Tertiary industry is the largest group of industries in MEDCs. It involves a wide range of services — anything from teaching, nursing and retailing to the police force or the civil service and transport.

Quaternary Industry is Research and Development

Quaternary industry is where scientists and researchers investigate and develop new products to sell. Quaternary industry is the newest and smallest industrial sector, but it's growing rapidly due to developments in information technology and communication.

Quaternary industry

EXAM TIP
Think of some examples of the different types of industry. Try to put them into a chain like the examples above. Remember, quaternary industry is less common than the others — it doesn't have to be part of the process unless the company needs new research.

Industry is Not the Same as Employment

Industry is part of a chain — from raw materials to finished product, finished product to service sector and service sector to research and development.

Employment is the job you do. So you could have a tertiary job as a secretary in a secondary industry like a toy factory.

Employment Structure Varies in LEDCs, NICs and MEDCs

LEDCs, NICs (Newly Industrialised Countries — see page 46) and MEDCs all have different employment structures.

LEDCs tend to have more people working in primary industries because an industrial sector hasn't developed.

NICs normally have lots of people working in secondary industries. This is because foreign investment has developed secondary industries.

MEDCs usually have more people working in tertiary industry because the economy is developed and there are a high number of jobs in service industries.

Changing Industry — MEDCs

Section Three
People and their Needs

Industry in MEDCs has changed a lot in the last 50 years for a variety of reasons.

Traditional Manufacturing has Declined and the Service Sector has Grown

Raw materials have started to run out
Many natural resources have been used up and others are too expensive to continue extracting. Some materials are now imported from abroad.

Competition from other countries has increased
Many countries like LEDCs manufacture goods at cheaper costs than MEDCs can. This is often due to lower wages and poorer working conditions as well as less strict pollution controls.

EXAMPLES

The coal belt across the West Midlands has been exhausted. This means that the coal mining industry no longer exists in the area (e.g. in Derbyshire and Staffordshire).

This has Two Effects on Industrial Location

Many industries have relocated near ports where raw materials are imported.

New tertiary industries are often footloose, meaning they are not tied to a raw material location, and locate in pleasant environments near transport routes and near the markets (e.g. hi-tech industries like computing).

The Service Sector is now the Largest Employer

Increases in tertiary industries mean that manufacturing employs a smaller proportion of the working population. The pie charts show the change in the UK. The decline in numbers working in manufacturing is also due to the increase in mechanisation and robots in factories.

Employment change in the UK from 1945 to 1995

EXAMPLES

Many companies (e.g. HSBC) have moved their call centres to places like Delhi in India, where running costs are cheaper.

The Government Affects Industrial Location in the UK

The British government is trying to change industry in four ways:

- Setting up industrial areas (trading estates) and enterprise zones to encourage new industrial and commercial businesses.
- Encouraging companies to set up where there's high unemployment by giving incentives like cheap rent.
- Encouraging the development of derelict areas, e.g. Docklands of London.
- Encouraging foreign investment into the UK.

Footloose Industries often Locate in Science Parks

Science parks are estates of modern, usually footloose industries such as pharmaceuticals and computing which have grown up in recent years on the outskirts of towns. There are 3 main reasons for their growth:

The need to be near raw material has been replaced by the need to be near research centres like universities and similar industries. Developments in hi-tech industry happen fast so companies need to be up-to-date to survive.

Land is often cheaper on the town outskirts than in the traditional central industrial areas, and access to transport routes is better.

Information technology is increasingly allowing hi-tech industry to locate further away from heavily populated areas.

EXAMPLES

Science parks
Silicon Glen, Scotland
Cambridge Science Park, Cambridge

**Section Three
People and their Needs**

Changing Industry — LEDCs

The characteristics of industry in LEDCs are different from those in MEDCs.

Industry in an LEDC can be Formal or Informal

The formal sector is regular waged employment, usually manufacturing. Wages are often low and hours can be long, but it provides a regular income.

The informal sector is usually work in small scale manufacturing or service industries — where people create their own employment to meet local demand.

In many LEDCs, more people look for work in the formal sector than there are jobs. So the informal sector plays a vital role in the economy of many countries, employing more people than the formal sector.

There is little or no security in the informal sector, and many people are trapped by lack of opportunity to improve their position.

LEDCs have found it difficult to develop their formal sector, because they don't have the money to invest in it, and lack the infrastructure (power supplies and transport networks) necessary for success.

EXAMPLES

Formal sector	Breweries Clothes manufacturers
Informal sector	Tourist guides Food sellers Shoe cleaners

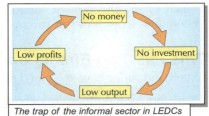
The trap of the informal sector in LEDCs

Some LEDCs are now Newly Industrialised Countries

Not all LEDCs share the same characteristics as those described above. Countries like the Pacific Rim countries in South East Asia are a separate case.

The Pacific Rim countries have seen dramatic levels of industrialisation in the last few decades, so they're called Newly Industrialised Countries (NICs).

The greatest level of industrialisation has occurred in South Korea, Taiwan, Hong Kong and Singapore — collectively known as Tiger Economies.

Singapore's built-up skyline

Although circumstances in each country are different, they share several characteristics which have helped this development:

- They invested in infrastructure during the 1960s.
- They have a motivated and cheap work force which attracted American and Japanese investors.
- They invested money very cleverly in new high-tech products.
- They have a large population which is a home market for the goods.

As a result, LEDCs have become fierce competition to the manufacturing industries of MEDCs.

There have been some negative consequences for industrialising LEDCs. The manufacturing industry has caused a lot of air pollution. People's health can be damaged because of poor working conditions in factories. Also, relying on foreign investment means that economies are unstable when there are recessions.

EXAM TIP
Remember Hong Kong is not an independent country — it's part of China.

WORLD LOCATION

area of NICs

ASIAN NIC LOCATION

Case Study

Section Three
People and their Needs

This case study looks at the causes and consequences of <u>industrialisation</u> in Brazil.

Case Study: <u>Brazil — A Newly Industrialised Country</u>

Lots of <u>factors</u> make Brazil <u>attractive</u> to investors:

- Brazil is a large country with a <u>large population</u>. This means that there is a very big potential workforce and a high demand for manufactured goods.
- 75% of Brazil's population live in urban areas so the majority of the workforce is in reach of <u>urban industries</u>.
- Brazil has large reserves of <u>raw materials</u> such as iron ore, tin and uranium.
- The Brazilian government has deliberately encouraged foreign companies to <u>invest</u> in Brazil.
- Foreign companies like Ford, Volkswagen and Pepsi have been attracted by <u>cheap labour costs</u>.
- Brazilian industries are able to supply a large domestic market as well as <u>exporting</u> to the rest of South America and USA.

WORLD LOCATION

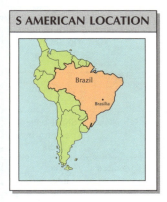
S AMERICAN LOCATION

There are <u>negative</u> and <u>positive</u> consequences:

Many different companies have moved their manufacturing to Brazil. The increase in manufacturing has caused a lot of change in Brazil.

Negative consequences:

- High demand for energy supplies has led to <u>fossil fuel shortage</u>.
- The <u>rainforests</u> are being <u>destroyed</u> due to the high demand for mining, HEP and ranching.
- Many people have moved from rural areas to urban areas to find jobs. The cities have become <u>overpopulated</u> so <u>squatter settlements</u> have developed.
- Increased industry has led to <u>air pollution</u> and <u>traffic congestion</u>.

Problems of industrialisation

FACT

A company from an MEDC which manufactures its goods in an LEDC or an NIC is known as a multinational corporation (MNC) or a transnational corporation (TNC).

Rising standard of living

Positive consequences:

- <u>New towns</u> have been created in areas where industries have been developed.
- Many people have experienced a <u>rising standard of living</u> due to the wealth created by new industries.
- The government has been able to use the profits of industrialisation to <u>improve run-down areas</u>.
- New industries have helped to <u>reduce</u> levels of <u>unemployment</u>.
- The government has developed <u>HEP</u> (hydro-electric power) to meet energy demands and <u>92%</u> of the country's electricity is now supplied in this way.

**Section Three
People and their Needs**

Classifying Farming

The term farming applies to a wide variety of activities, from a smallholding run by one family to vast plantations covering hundreds of square miles.

Farms can be Classified by Produce

Arable farms specialise in growing crops.

Pastoral farms specialise in rearing animals.

Arable farming

Pastoral farming

Mixed farms are both pastoral and arable.

EXAMPLES	
Types of farm:	
Arable	Crop farms in East Anglia
Pastoral	Dairy farms in Devon
Intensive	Rice farming in South East Asia
Extensive	Wheat prairies in Canada
Subsistence	Small-scale rice growing in India
Commercial	Market gardening in the Netherlands

Farms can be Classified by Input

Intensive crop farming

Intensive farms involve a high level of input to achieve a high yield per hectare. This input can either be technology, as in market gardening (fertilisers, greenhouses, machines) or labour, as in rice farming in South East Asia (high number of workers per hectare).

Extensive farms have low input and low output per hectare. High yield is produced by covering large areas of often low grade land, but with few workers. Examples include the wheat prairies of Canada and the Pampas cattle ranches of South America.

Extensive animal farming

Farms can be Classified by Purpose

Some people farm to earn money, others produce plants and animals to feed themselves and their families.

Subsistence farming

Subsistence farms are those where produce is mainly grown for the use of the farmer. A surplus (extra to requirements) may be sold to buy other goods. Although many subsistence farmers are very poor, this is not always the case.

EXAM TIP

Shifting cultivation is a type of subsistence farming where a farmer uses an area for a short time, before moving on, leaving the land to recover. Land can be left for 20 years or more before farming is resumed.

Commercial farms are those in which the produce is grown for sale. These include plantation agriculture (huge farms growing cash crops) and factory farming (animals kept at high density in small units).

Commercial crop farm

Farms can Fall into More Than One Category

Most types of farming will fall into several of these categories — for example, hill farming in Wales is pastoral, extensive and commercial. Rice farming in northern India is arable, intensive and subsistence.

Distribution of Farming Types

Section Three — People and their Needs

Farming depends on the physical characteristics of an area — the climate, soils and relief. Different farming types are associated with different areas, on a global and regional scale.

The Farming Type Depends on the Climate

On a global scale, patterns of farming are associated with climatic belts — with distinct differences between the temperate and tropical climatic zones.

The temperate latitudes have mainly commercial farming — most of the countries involved are MEDCs — and their produce includes cereals, livestock and mixed farming. Intensive and extensive farming are found here.

The tropical latitudes have both commercial and subsistence farming, and mostly include LEDCs. Plantations are also important in tropical areas, e.g. tea and cocoa beans.

Areas of extreme climate (either hot or cold) have little sedentary (fixed) farming, but nomadic hunters or herders are found.

EXAMPLES
Farming in different climates

Climate	Example
Temperate	Intensive horticulture in NW Europe; Extensive sheep farming in Australia
Tropical	Coffee and sugar plantations in Brazil
Extreme	Tuareg herders of Sub-Saharan Africa; Inuit of north Canada

Rainfall and Relief Affect Farming on a Regional Scale

Patterns of farming can be identified within countries due to variations in rainfall and relief — the causes are demonstrated by the patterns evident in the UK:

Western UK receives more relief rainfall due to its upland areas and prevailing westerly winds — the east has less rainfall, is flatter, and has a longer growing season. Farms in the south and east are more intensive, have larger fields and use more machinery than those in the north and west. This results in the distribution shown below. Remember that there are more types of farming in the UK than this, but there is a clear general pattern by region.

SUMMARY
Physical and human factors that affect farming:

PHYSICAL
- climate
- weather
- relief
- soils

HUMAN
- money
- labour
- government influences (e.g. quotas)
- nearness to markets
- transport
- farmer's decisions

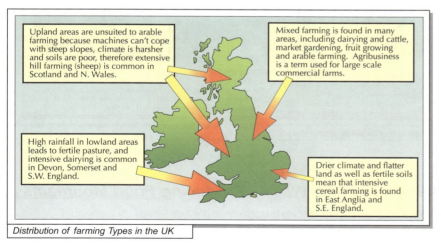

Distribution of farming Types in the UK

- Upland areas are unsuited to arable farming because machines can't cope with steep slopes, climate is harsher and soils are poor, therefore extensive hill farming (sheep) is common in Scotland and N. Wales.
- Mixed farming is found in many areas, including dairying and cattle, market gardening, fruit growing and arable farming. Agribusiness is a term used for large scale commercial farms.
- High rainfall in lowland areas leads to fertile pasture, and intensive dairying is common in Devon, Somerset and S.W. England.
- Drier climate and flatter land as well as fertile soils mean that intensive cereal farming is found in East Anglia and S.E. England.

Economic and Political Issues also Affect Farming

Physical characteristics are not the only influence on farming types, but they do dictate what type of farming is possible. Economic and political influences are also important, e.g. nearness to market and government quotas.

Section Three
People and their Needs

Farming in the European Union (EU)

The Common Agricultural Policy (CAP) governs farming in all countries in the EU. It was set up after World War II to increase European food production by making farming more modern and efficient.

A CAP Target is to Increase Farming Efficiency

The CAP introduced subsidies to encourage a complementary production of crops, i.e. the EU as a whole produced the right amount of each crop. This was intended to make the system more efficient by avoiding the problem of shortfalls in particular crops.

However, encouraging farmers to increase their yields led to environmental problems. There was an increase in chemical fertilisers and pesticides, which presented a threat to wildlife. And there are other problems:

Over 25% of UK Hedgerows Have been Removed Since 1945

Farmers in arable areas use large and expensive machinery because it is more efficient. This has resulted in the removal of hedgerows for three reasons:

- Larger fields make turning huge machinery easier.
- Land used for hedgerows can be brought into cultivation — increasing yield.
- Hedgerows take time and money to maintain, and harbour pests and weeds.

All these factors encouraged farmers to remove hedgerows from their fields. But concern has been increasing over this for the reasons shown in the diagram.

> **EXAMPLE**
> Many hedgerows have been removed from eastern counties, such as Norfolk and Kent, where arable farming dominates.

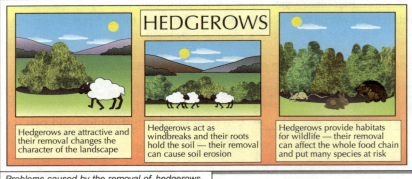

Problems caused by the removal of hedgerows

CAP Worked Too Well — Producing Food Mountains

After World War II farmers were given subsidies (assistance money) to encourage them to produce more.

The EU guaranteed a standard price for farmers' products regardless of market forces or the price of the same product outside Europe — this protected the farmers from cheap imports from abroad.

The subsidies and guaranteed prices meant the EU farmers ended up damaging the environment and producing too much food — gluts of butter, grain, milk and wine called food mountains. The surplus food had to be stored and later destroyed, costing huge amounts of money.

> **FACT**
> Many people think it's wasteful to have huge stocks of food in Europe when people in poorer parts of the world are starving. Sometimes food stocks are given to poorer regions as aid.

Farming in the European Union (EU)

Section Three — People and their Needs

The EU tried four different things to solve the problems of over-production.

The EU Introduced Quotas to Reduce Milk Production

The UK joined the EU in 1973. Quotas were imposed in 1984 to control milk production across Europe, limiting the amount of milk each farmer was allowed to produce.

Fines were set for milk produced over this limit, creating two difficulties:

- The quotas were based on a production level below the current one — so some farmers had to reduce their milk production.
- The quota level didn't take into account any expansion of farmers' dairy herds, so if a herd was below normal size (e.g. because of illness) this lowered the production level automatically. When the herd grew, the farm would overproduce.

> **FACT**
>
> Farmers can increase their quota by buying another farm or another farmer's quota. But this is expensive and can put them out of business — they don't know if or when the EU will change the quotas in the future, and this makes planning difficult.

Set-aside was Introduced to Reduce Food Production

Set-aside means the EU pays farmers a subsidy to leave land uncultivated to reduce overall production. It began as a voluntary scheme in 1988, but by 1992 there was still a surplus of cereals being produced.

In order to continue receiving EU subsidies, all farms with over 20 hectares of land must now leave 15% of it as set-aside. It should be left for at least five years, and though they can't farm it, they can use it for other purposes.

> **FACT**
>
> Alternative uses for set-aside land:
> - woodland
> - wildlife areas — grants are available for these in some areas
> - fallow land — land is left uncultivated and a grant is paid to the farmer

Diversification Schemes Use Farmland for Other Things

Diversification is when farmers develop other business activities in addition to their traditional ones. The aim of farm diversification is to:

- reduce farm surpluses — to prevent food mountains.
- cater for the increased demand for leisure activities in rural areas.
- reduce the damage to the environment caused by modern farming.

Farms now have a range of land uses. In addition to traditional farming duties, farms often provide other services and leisure opportunities to boost their income:

Farm land uses

- rare breeds, specialist centres and pets' corners.
- adventure playgrounds and nature trails.
- tea shops and craft shops.
- bed and breakfast and holiday accommodation.
- pony trekking and horse riding.

Hobby farming is a term for specialist farms centred around the farmer's interest (e.g. a rare breed or plant) — these have potential as visitor centres and can broaden the farmer's income.

> **EXAM TIP**
>
> The rural-urban fringe of big cities is accessible for large numbers of people, so these extra activities are more common here than in remote areas. However, farm holidays in mountain and scenic areas are also popular.

ESAs were Set Up

Environmentally Sensitive Areas (ESAs) were set up in the early 1990s as a result of increasing pressure by conservationists to protect the environment.

Farmers in these areas can obtain subsidies if they farm in an 'environmentally friendly' way. This means things like using organic farming with traditional farming methods — like using horses instead of tractors, using manure and not chemicals, and using dry-stone walls and hedgerows.

> **EXAMPLE**
>
> The Cotswold Hills and the Yorkshire Dales are designated ESAs.

Section Three
People and their Needs

Location of Industry

The growth of cities, population distribution and social and employment changes have all been affected by the location of industry. This page and the next page describe the four big influences on the location of industry — raw materials, labour supply, transport and the market.

Raw Materials Influence *Industrial Location*

During the Industrial Revolution, new industries needed power supplies (originally fast-flowing streams) and raw materials such as coal or iron ore. Industry grew up where these were easily available.

A pattern of industrial location developed where different areas specialised in industries using local resources. As most of our natural resources are in the north of England, this became our industrial heartland.

Location near raw materials reduces transport costs, particularly if they are bulky or lose weight during the manufacturing process.

Ports became important too, as they were the source of imported raw materials.

EXAMPLES
Locations of industry:
Local resources
South Wales — coal
Sheffield — steel (particularly cutlery)
Newcastle — ship building
Ports
Liverpool, Bristol

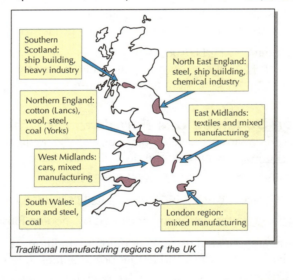

Traditional manufacturing regions of the UK

Labour Supply has Influenced *Industrial Location*

Availability of labour supply is important to industry. A factory is likely to locate where there are enough people looking for work to fill their needs. Unemployment varies enormously by region, so this can be an important factor. The labour supply must be suitable. There are three main types of labour requirement:

- A large pool of unskilled labour — some industries will train their own workforce in the necessary skills, and simply need a large group of available people.

- A large specialised workforce — some industries need a large workforce with particular skills, and they will often locate near similar industries, as the workforce will meet this requirement.

- A small highly skilled workforce — some industries need highly skilled or qualified staff, and will need to locate where these people are available.

Labour costs also vary around the country, so industries try to locate in an area where they can keep these costs down. Industries requiring highly skilled workers are less likely to be able to do this.

EXAMPLES	
Workforce requirements	
Unskilled labour	Processed food manufacturer
Specialised workforce	Car manufacturer
Highly skilled workforce	Scientific research laboratories

Location of Industry

Section Three — People and their Needs

This page covers more factors that affect the location of industry.

Transport Influences Location in *Three Ways*

The cost of transporting raw materials and finished product:
If the raw materials cost more to transport than the finished product (they may produce a lot of waste during manufacture, for instance) it is cheaper to locate near the raw materials.

If the finished product is more expensive to transport (it may take up more space, or be expensive to insure) then the cheaper location will be nearer the market.

The type of transport used:
Traditionally, bulky cargo was transported by rail, so rail links were important. The increase in road transport in recent years has changed this. Many industries are now located near main roads, particularly motorway intersections. Small high value items can be transported by air, but this is expensive. Goods destined for overseas markets are transported by ship, often using container lorries and roll-on roll-off ferries.

The speed required:
Some products need to be transported quickly, possibly because they go off quickly (e.g. milk). This may require a more expensive form of transport.

SUMMARY

Transport options

ROAD - convenient, flexible, specialist vehicles available, traffic jams a problem.

RAIL - cheaper, slower, suitable for heavy cargo, restricted routes.

SEA - cheaper, slower, only suited for international transport. Good for specialist cargo, e.g. oil.

AIR - expensive, fast, suitable for small high value items.

The *Market* Influences Industrial Location

The market is where a product is sold — usually a lot of separate places.

Location near the market is best when transporting the product is expensive. For some UK industries who export to Europe, a location in southern England has become attractive.

When products are sent on from one industry to another it helps to be located close by. This leads to industrial agglomeration.

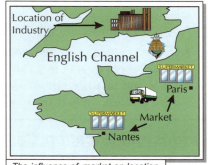
The influence of market on location

KEY TERM

Industrial agglomeration: A concentration of linked industry in one area.

An agglomeration needs lots of labour in the region.
A skilled labour force attracts more industries to the area.
This means that labour pools and markets are often found in the same place.

Other Factors Influence Industrial Location too

Some industries are heavily reliant on large amounts of energy. These industries should be close to the energy source, or in a suitable location to receive imports.

Finance affects the location of industry — the cost of land varies from place to place. Also, more capital is needed for the larger industries.

Physical site affects the location of industry because some types of industry need particular sites, e.g. large factories need to be built on large, flat areas.

Another important factor is government policy. The government will encourage certain types of industry according to the social and economic conditions at the time.

Section Three
People and their Needs

Case Studies

You need to learn all four case studies on this page — two are on <u>farming</u> and two are on <u>location of industry</u>.

Farming Case Studies:
Case Study 1: <u>Dairy Farming on the Cheshire Plain, UK</u>

The weather and landscape of the Cheshire Plain is ideal for raising cattle. There are <u>mild winters</u> and <u>warm summers</u> with a <u>gentle relief</u>.

Mild temperatures, high rainfall and fertile soils provide good <u>growing conditions</u> for grass, which provides food for the cattle. The commercial farms are large and well equipped with buildings and machinery.

Dairy farming in Cheshire isn't labour intensive and there is a <u>high output</u> of milk and meat. The EU <u>quota</u> system means that farmers must not produce too much milk or they will be fined. <u>CAP</u> ensures that the farmers a paid a set price for the milk they produce.

Case Study 2: <u>Rice Growing in India</u>

Farming in India is based on a <u>monsoon climate.</u> During the summer India experiences very high precipitation. In the winter it is drier because winds blow from the land to the sea, so the clouds don't carry much moisture.

The <u>inputs</u> are flat land, soil, labour, rice seeds, animal manure, high temperatures and high rainfall. The <u>processes</u> that take place are ploughing, planting and harvesting. The <u>outputs</u> of the farm are the rice and the rice seeds.

A number of factors make farming in India <u>difficult</u>:
- The <u>soil</u> is poor quality, with not many nutrients.
- There is little <u>land</u> available to grow rice for the increasing population.
- Farmers are <u>poor</u> so they cannot afford many tools or seeds.

Rice is a <u>staple</u> food in India and it is grown as a <u>subsistence</u> crop by families and small communities. If the rice crop fails people will go hungry because there is often no alternative source of nutrition.

Industrial Location Case Studies:
Case Study 1: <u>Nissan in Washington</u>

<u>Nissan</u> is a <u>Japanese</u> car firm. They set up an <u>assembly plant</u> in Washington near Sunderland in N.E. England because the government offered them incentives. Lots of other factors made Washington <u>attractive</u> to Nissan:
- There are <u>good communication links</u> to the rest of the UK and EU.
- There was a <u>greenfield site</u> available next to the A19 with space for expansion meaning that Nissan could build a factory to meet their needs.
- The <u>wage costs</u> for labour are <u>cheaper</u> in the UK than in Japan.

Case Study 2: <u>Argos Distribution in the UK</u>

<u>Argos</u> is one of the UK's leading retailers. Argos has <u>13</u> warehouses and distribution centres in the UK including Stafford and Marston Gate (Bedfordshire). The <u>distribution centres</u> are all located in areas that are suited to the needs of the industry. They all have easy access to the national motorway and rail network.

Most of the distribution centres are located near the centre of the UK so they can access lots of different places easily and quickly. The distribution centres are all near large towns or cities so there is an <u>accessible labour force</u>.

UK LOCATION — Cheshire

WORLD LOCATION — INDIA

FACT: In places where there is not enough flat land available, terraces are constructed for growing rice.

UK LOCATION — Washington

The Leisure Industry

Section Three
People and their Needs

People in MEDCs have increasing amounts of spare time, which means that the leisure industry is growing quickly.

Leisure is a *Growing Industry*

Nowadays people have more <u>free time</u> — because the working week is shorter than it was 40 years ago. New laws give workers the right to a minimum number of days' holiday per year.

<u>Flexible working hours</u> mean people take time off at different times, while old attitudes that Sunday was a day of rest have changed.

At the same time, <u>wages have risen</u> at a higher rate than the cost of living — so people have <u>more money</u> to spend.

The leisure industry <u>caters</u> for people's need to relax and do things they enjoy, but also <u>creates new activities</u> e.g. kite surfing.

Examples include the <u>leisure centres</u> and <u>fitness clubs</u> that have grown up in towns to provide for the growing market.

The definition of leisure is changing — many people now see education and shopping as leisure activities rather than necessary tasks.

Increased leisure time

EXAMPLE
Many people now think of shopping as a leisure activity rather than a necessity. Huge shopping malls have been built to meet the increased demand for shopping. Examples include:

Place	Mall
Sheffield	Meadowhall
Manchester	Trafford Centre
Gateshead	Metro Centre
Birmingham	Bull Ring

Tourism — an *Expanding* Leisure *Industry*

People are taking <u>longer</u> and more <u>expensive</u> holidays:
- People have more <u>disposable income</u> nowadays.
- Most jobs give at least three weeks of <u>paid holiday time</u> per year — many as much as five weeks.
- Many people now have <u>more than one</u> holiday each year.
- Travel has become <u>cheaper</u>, particularly air travel.
- <u>Jet aircraft</u> have made all parts of the world easily accessible.

<u>Tourism</u> has become a huge industry all over the world. It provides a huge amount of the <u>money</u> countries need for things like schools, hospitals and roads.

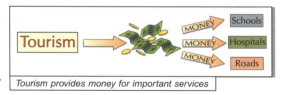
Tourism provides money for important services

EXAMPLES

LEDC holiday destinations
Goa
The Gambia
Kenya

Specialist holidays
Safari
Sailing
Skiing
Cruise

People want to Try New Kinds of Holiday

People are <u>increasingly aware</u> of new holiday destinations and are keen to visit unusual places.

They have become <u>more adventurous</u> and have <u>higher expectations</u> — people whose parents might have gone to Blackpool may now prefer two weeks in the Caribbean sun.

Better than Blackpool

There are now <u>specialist activity holidays</u>, e.g. bird-watching or cycling holidays.

<u>LEDCs</u> want a share of the <u>huge profits</u> of this industry — they promote themselves as <u>holiday destinations</u> to fund <u>development</u>, and they have the benefit of being <u>much cheaper</u> than many MEDC destinations.

Section Three — People and their Needs

Tourism and LEDCs

Tourism is becoming more and more important in LEDCs.
In some LEDCs it's become their main industry.

Tourism is one Route to Development

Tourism brings foreign money into the LEDC, along with new investment — big companies build hotels and airports to profit from the tourist trade.

There are new jobs for the people, and local businesses are strengthened.

There can be a knock-on effect — other industries start to move to the LEDC as the infrastructure develops and labour costs are still cheaper than in MEDCs.

EXAMPLES
Tourism brings new jobs for local people in hotels, shops, restaurants and as tour guides.
Local farmers will also have an improved income by being able to supply food to hotels.

Game Parks are Wildlife Preservation Areas

Safaris are popular holiday destinations in LEDCs like Kenya, Tanzania and India.

The animals in game parks can be seen in their natural state — they are a huge attraction for visitors.

People are also attracted to the scenery in game parks — lakes and waterfalls are popular recreational sites.

Accommodation is often in tents and traditional buildings rather than conventional hotels.

Lion in his natural environment

EXAMPLES

Game parks
- Masai Mara game reserve, Kenya
- Zambezi national park, Zimbabwe

Game park recreation
- Safaris
- Hot air balloon flights
- Water sports on lakes, like lake Nakuru in Kenya

Tourism has Several Disadvantages

Building basic infrastructure is expensive, especially road and sewage systems.

Many of the profits go abroad — flights are arranged and paid for abroad, and hotels are often owned by multinational companies.

Increased wealth is restricted to the local area. The rest of the country stays poor.

Local customs and culture may be exploited or disappear.

Mass tourism is not sustainable (it damages the environment) and in the end people will become fed up with the crowds, pollution, spoilt beaches and sewage and they'll find somewhere else to go.

Ecotourism Reduces the Effect of Tourists

Ecotourism is a recent idea — specialist holidays for small groups living in reserve zones, eating local food and using simple local accommodation, allowing them to get really close to nature. Unlike mass tourism, ecotourism aims to be sustainable — causing as little impact as possible.

- Small group numbers means they can enter sensitive areas that others can't.
- These holidays are more expensive, so the income for the LEDC is better.
- Groups are conservation-minded and follow strict guidelines.
- Local culture and customs are respected.

EXAMPLE
Ecotourism is popular in places where there is lots of unusual wildlife. For example people take boating eco-trips on the Amazon river through the Brazilian rainforest.

Tourism in Peru is a Good Example of Tourism in LEDCs

Most tourists visit Peru to explore the Andes mountains and discover the Inca settlements. Tourism brings money to the area, but must be managed carefully.

WORLD LOCATION
Peru

Inca settlement

There are guidelines in place as to how the area can be used by tourists — in this way, it can be protected for future generations. Tourism in Peru has benefited the locals, as many have been able to get well-paid jobs in the tourist industry and tourists can buy their handicrafts. Tourism in Peru has also benefited the country as a whole because it has raised its profile and increased the amount of money being spent in the country.

Tourism and Conflict

Section Three
People and their Needs

Pretty much everything people do causes conflict somewhere along the line — tourism is just the same. Learn why for your exams.

Tourist <u>Demands</u> Cause <u>Conflict</u> in MEDCs

Tourism depends on natural and human resources to attract people to an area. Demand for <u>access</u> to tourist areas increases <u>road construction</u> and <u>building</u> of other facilities, often on farmland or open spaces.

<u>Job-providing industries</u> like quarrying can <u>ruin</u> a <u>landscape</u> that attracts tourists.

<u>Residents</u> in tourist areas like national parks might want new <u>facilities</u> like supermarkets and shopping centres which visitors and planners may think are <u>not in keeping</u> with the area.

<u>Open land</u> is often seen as <u>recreation space</u>, but it also provides <u>farmers' livelihoods</u>.

Some <u>recreational activities</u> are <u>incompatible</u> and can't happen together.

EXAMPLES

Human Resources	Natural Resources
Transport links	Warm sunshine
Culture	Snow
Architecture	Sandy beaches
Museums	Mountains

EXAMPLE

The use of Lake Windermere and its shores for quiet walks, water-skiing, yachting and angling is a good example of incompatible recreational activities — they can't all happen at once without certain user groups becoming annoyed.

Conflict-causing events in MEDC tourist areas

<u>Conflict</u> in LEDCs comes from <u>Tourist Development</u>

LEDCs promote tourism in game parks, but <u>too many visitors</u> can ruin the wild animals' <u>natural habitat</u> so the animals are forced to move to a new area.

Developments to accommodate tourists can also cause conflict because natural habitats are destroyed when facilities like hotels are built.

The <u>demand for food</u> by tourists can also cause conflict because sometimes farmers are forced to expand their farms into conservation areas and destroy <u>natural habitats</u>. Problems can be caused if animals from game parks damage local farmers' land.

LEDC <u>Cultures</u> are often Challenged by Tourism

Tourists bring their <u>own culture</u> with them and often <u>don't respect</u> the culture they're visiting. Often MEDC women <u>dress</u> and <u>act</u> in a way that <u>offends</u> the people of the LEDC — especially in <u>Islamic countries</u> where it is usual for women to cover their skin in public.

<u>MEDC tourists</u> are seen as being <u>rich</u> — and some <u>LEDC people</u> have this as a <u>goal</u>. Lots of people in LEDCs <u>copy</u> foreign attitudes to try to <u>achieve</u> this goal. <u>Development</u> encourages <u>changing attitudes</u> — indigenous cultures <u>change</u> or <u>disappear</u> as locals adopt the practices of tourists from MEDCs.

Local women cover up

Tourists can offend locals

FACT

The introduction of western products like Coca-Cola and McDonalds to LEDCs is part of the process known as <u>globalisation</u>.

<u>Sustainable Tourism</u> is Growing in Popularity

Tourism that involves <u>local</u> people is less likely to cause conflict. It's important that local people have a say in the way the tourist industry is developed. The impact of tourism on the environment can be reduced by careful <u>planning</u> and <u>controlling</u> visitor numbers and activities. Special areas like <u>national parks</u> also make sure that land can be managed in a <u>sustainable</u> way.

TIP

There's more about sustainable tourism in the ecotourism section on page 56.

Section Three
People and their Needs

Case Studies

Sustainable tourism meets the needs of today without damaging the environment and creating problems in the future. The following case studies give an LEDC and MEDC example of trying to develop sustainable tourism.

Case Study 1: Ecotourism in Belize (LEDC)

Belize is a small country in Central America. It is an attractive tourist destination because it has beautiful scenery and beaches. Many tourists travel to Belize to see its barrier reef and wide variety of plant and animal life.

The government of Belize is trying to make sure that the natural environment is not damaged. There are many National Parks and reserves. They have banned farming in some areas to prevent erosion. Local people are very involved in tourist development and it is planned that in the future they will be in complete control. The tourism that is introduced is designed to improve the local area and the lives of local people rather than cause damage.

Visitors to Belize are asked to follow a set of guidelines to make sure they don't cause any damage. The list below shows some of the guidelines:

- Belize relies on collection of rainwater for its drinking water — guests are asked to restrict their water use, e.g. by taking short showers.

- Tourists who go diving must not touch or remove any of the coral. All guides have training about protecting the reef so they can check tourists don't cause damage.

- Don't trample delicate plants in the rainforest.

- All waste must be safely disposed of.

- Don't buy souvenirs which are made from animal products.

- Be quiet and respectful around churches.

Case Study 2: Lake District National Park, UK (MEDC)

The Lake District is in north-west England. It is one of the UK's national parks — a protected area of land, preserved for the enjoyment and education of people.

Tourists come to enjoy the scenery and the natural beauty of the mountainous area with its glacial features, large natural lakes and interesting species of wildlife. The national park also provides many activities for people to take part in, including bird watching, rambling, pony-trekking, rock-climbing, boat rides, sailing and other water sports.

There are lots of demands on the environment, so there are lots of conflicts:

Lake District scenery

- Water companies conflict with farmers over flooding valley floor farmland. They also conflict with conservationists over ruining the countryside, and tourists who want to use the water for leisure activities.

- Farmers conflict with roadbuilders who use up valuable land, and tourists who drop litter, leave farm gates open and damage dry-stone walls.

- Conservationists conflict with tourists over damaging natural features by footpath erosion, needing tourist accommodation building, dropping litter, etc.

The national park authorities have to balance out the various uses and demands without destroying the scenery that is the major attraction in the first place.

Energy and Power

Section Three: People and their Needs

From burning wood for warmth, to solar-powered calculators — humans need energy. We get it from natural resources converted into power supplies at power stations — usually in the form of electricity or gas.

Energy Resources are Renewable or Non-Renewable

Non-renewable resources take so long to form that they can't be replaced once they run out. These include fossil fuels — oil, coal and gas — which have traditionally supplied most of our energy. They are not sustainable and are a major source of pollution.

Renewable resources are sustainable resources that won't run out, e.g. water, wind, and the sun. Wood can be renewable too, if replanting is managed well.

LEDCs rely more heavily on wood as fuel. This is becoming a problem — population growth means increased demand on fuel, and leads to deforestation as more trees are cut down. This can also contribute to soil erosion and flooding as the earth loses tree cover protection.

There's an important link between energy and development — MEDCs represent 25% of the world's population, but consume 80% of the world's energy supplies. If LEDCs used as much as MEDCs, we'd have a huge environmental problem.

Alternative Sources of Energy are being Developed

As fossil fuels begin to run out, alternative energy sources are being adopted:

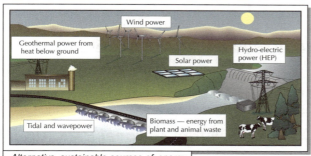

Alternative, sustainable sources of energy

EXAMPLES

Energy source	Location
Wind	Cumbria, UK
Geothermal	Iceland
Solar	California, USA
Tidal	France
HEP	Tucurui, Brazil

These energy sources are renewable, but at the moment there are two big problems with their use:

- Alternative energy sources can't produce as much power as fossil fuel power stations without being gigantic.
- They can be very expensive to set up and maintain.

Use of Nuclear Power has Recently Increased

This has caused debate over its advantages as a cheaper and cleaner form of power than fossil fuels, and the disadvantages of the potential serious risks to people and the environment from radiation leaks and the dumping of nuclear waste products. People sometimes have very strong opinions about the issue, but you need to be balanced and remember both sides.

There are Three Major Issues in the Energy Debate

- It's important to balance the need for power and the need to protect the environment from pollution.
- Technology must be developed to help find and improve the use of alternative energy sources.
- Energy use in general must become more efficient, so that less is wasted.

EXAMPLES

Current sources of the world's energy supplies:

Energy source	% of world energy production
Oil	31%
Coal	23%
Natural gas	21%
Biomass (e.g. wood)	13%
HEP	6%
Nuclear	5.9%
Others	0.1%

Section Three — People and their Needs

Effects of Changing Resources

This page focuses on how a change in energy supply has a major effect on the economy and society.

Sources of Energy have Changed Over Time

As new methods of <u>energy production</u> have developed older methods have been gradually reduced.

In the past most UK power stations and industries used fossil fuels like coal to produce energy.

Over the last thirty years coal has become less popular — the government has turned to new energy sources like <u>nuclear power</u>, natural gas and <u>renewable energy sources</u> like wind power and HEP (hydro-electric power).

Some parts of the UK that are traditional coal mining areas have experienced decline whilst areas that are the site of new power developments often experience economic and social growth.

Renewable sources of energy are increasingly popular

FACT

In the future there will have to be changes in the sources of energy we use because the supplies of coal oil and gas are running out:

Resource	Approx. number of years left before it runs out
Oil	45
Coal	240
Natural gas	70

Development of Alternative Energy Brings Growth

Economic effects:
Areas which are used to develop new power sources often experience an <u>improved local economy</u> because skilled, affluent workers move into the area. New jobs for locals are created so there is more money in the <u>local economy</u>. In the past the UK government was keen to develop <u>new power stations</u> so they injected a lot of <u>money</u> into the projects to ensure they were successful.

Social effects:
New job opportunities means that <u>unemployment often falls</u> in the surrounding area. <u>More money</u> in the local economy means villages and towns nearby tend to benefit. Existing businesses (e.g. builders and hotels) can benefit directly from <u>new developments</u>. More people moving to the area means a rising population which can lead to <u>improved facilities and housing</u>.

FACT

Nuclear power stations were very popular in the 60s and 70s. They were often built in deprived areas, e.g. Sellafield near Whitehaven in Cumbria. Many locals in these areas were keen for the power stations to be built because they provided an injection of cash and jobs into the local economy.

Closure of Traditional Power Stations Causes Decline

Economic effects:
Areas that had relied on a certain industry which then closes (e.g. coal mining areas) experience a sudden <u>drop in the local economy</u>. High rates of <u>unemployment</u> create a struggling local economy. Shops and businesses find it difficult to survive. People are forced to move away to look for work and this leads to <u>falling house prices</u>.

Social effects:
Areas often suffer from high rates of <u>unemployment</u> because of redundancies. Unemployment can lead to problems of social deprivation, such as <u>high crime rates</u>. Housing areas become run-down because of a <u>lack of money</u>. People move away to look for work so areas become <u>underpopulated</u>. People aren't keen to move into the area so buildings become <u>derelict</u> and unsafe.

Case Study

**Section Three
People and their Needs**

This case study looks at the consequences of a shift in energy supply for the town of Consett.

Case Study: Mine Closure in Consett, 1980

Consett was a traditional coal mining area

Consett is a small town in the northeast of England that developed around a deep-mined coalfield.

Traditionally the area has relied on heavy mining and heavy industries like steel making (which used a lot of the local coal) for employment.

Terraced housing for miners in Consett

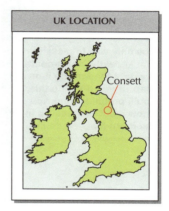
UK LOCATION — Consett

The coal mine and steel works in Consett were closed

In 1980 the coalmine and the town's steelworks were closed. The closures were due to competition from other areas and a shift in energy supply.

The closures had serious social and economic effects on the local community.

- Unemployment rose from 15% to 27%. This made Consett one of the worst areas for unemployment in England.
- The closures had negative effects on other local industries and businesses and the local economy struggled.
- Many people moved away to try and find employment.
- Crime rates rose and large parts of the town became run-down due to a lack of investment.

The government tried to improve the situation

The government and the local council tried to improve the situation by developing new industrial estates in Consett.

A new industrial estate was built on the site of an old colliery to try and attract new industries. The area has since experienced a shift away from primary industry. A lot of the new businesses are in the secondary sector (e.g. Derwent Valley Foods).
Some of the land around the collieries has new uses such as leisure and culture. For example the C2C (coast to coast) cycle route passes through Consett. Some sculptures made from steel which represent the industrial past of the area have been put up along the cycle route.

Efforts to improve the local economy have had some success and unemployment has fallen.

Despite these efforts the area has yet to recover fully from the closures of the coalmines and steel industry.

The C2C cycle route and a steel sculpture in Consett

Section Three
People and their Needs

Revision Summary

Time to see what you've learned and what you need to go over again.
Keep at it — it's hard work, but it'll all be worth it come the exam.

Development

1) What percentage of the world's population live in MEDCs?
2) What percentage of the world's wealth is owned by MEDCs?
3) What do LEDC and MEDC stand for?
4) Give one other name for LEDCs.
5) On the world map below, draw a line showing the north-south divide.

EXAM TIP

The only way to make sure you know the north-south divide is by drawing it on a map. If you don't do this, you'll probably think you know it but then realise in the exam that you don't.

6) Are the poorer countries mostly in the north or the south?
7) Why can GDP and GNP be misleading as indices of development?
8) Make a list of seven indices of development.
   What are the two main problems with the indices?

Classification of Industry

1) Write an exact definition of the four types of industry, and give two examples of each.
2) Place the following jobs under the correct heading: primary, secondary, tertiary or quaternary.
   Nurse, electrician, farmer, research scientist, fisherman, violin maker, double glazing salesman, car factory worker, coal miner, librarian, forestry worker, solicitor, taxi driver.
3) Give two reasons why traditional manufacturing has declined in MEDCs.
4) What is a 'footloose' industry?
5) Which industry has taken over from manufacturing as the largest employer in MEDCs?
6) What is the difference between formal and informal industry in LEDCs?
7) Give two reasons why many LEDCs have problems developing their industrial base.
8) What are NICs? What characteristics do they have which led them to become NICs?
9) Name two 'Tiger Economies'.
10) Make a table which shows the negative and positive consequences of industrialisation in Brazil.

EXAM TIP

Practise drawing sketch maps of case studies. If you annotate them with the details of the case study it'll help you remember the facts. You can also use the maps in your exam answers.

Revision Summary

Section Three
People and their Needs

Farming

1) What are: a) arable farms? b) pastoral farms? c) mixed farms?
2) Explain what is meant by the following:
   a) Intensive farms   b) Extensive farms
3) What are the characteristics of farming in
   a) tropical latitudes   b) temperate latitudes?
4) Sketch a rough map of the UK and mark on the main areas of hill sheep farming, mixed farming, dairying and intensive cereal farming.
5) Name four physical factors and six human factors that affect farming.
6) What does CAP stand for? When and why was the CAP set up?
7) What are food mountains, and how did the CAP cause them?
8) Name four methods used to reduce over-production in the EU?
9) Describe the land-use options for farmers involved in the set-aside scheme.
10) What is diversification? Give an example.

Industrial Location

1) Why do ports have an important influence on industrial location?
2) Give three ways in which labour supply influences the location of industry.
3) Write down three advantages and one disadvantage of road transport.
4) What is an industrial agglomeration?
5) How does the government affect industrial location?

Leisure and Tourism

1) Give two reasons why the leisure industry has grown.
2) Why are many people able to take more than one holiday a year?
3) What development has enabled people to take holidays abroad regularly?
4) Give three advantages that tourism brings to LEDCs.
5) List two reasons why tourism doesn't always benefit LEDCs.
6) What is a 'game park'? Name an example.
7) Explain how 'ecotourism' limits the impact of tourists on the environment.
8) List the main sources of conflict with tourism in MEDCs and LEDCs.
9) What guidelines do tourists in Belize have to follow?

Energy

1) What is the difference between renewable and non-renewable resources?
2) Name six ways we can use renewable resources to make electricity.
3) What are the pros and cons of nuclear power?
4) What are the three major issues in the energy debate?
5) Make a table which shows the problems that can be caused when traditional coal mines are closed.
6) Describe the problems found in Consett and how people have tried to tackle them.

> **EXAM TIP**
> Keep going through these questions until you can do them all without needing to look anything up. But once you can do them, don't ignore this section forever — keep coming back and checking you haven't forgotten it all.

Section Four
People & the Environment

Quarrying

The growing population and increasing standard of living is putting demands on the world's resources. A lot of quarrying is required to provide enough raw materials to meet demand. However, quarrying can often cause conflict.

Quarrying means Digging for Land Resources

Quarries spoil the landscape, and the land can't always be reclaimed.

Rock, sand and gravel are important resources, but to get at them a lot of unusable material has to be removed first.

Metal ores make up only a tiny fraction of the rocks in which they are found — the rest is waste. Other waste is dumped in quarries.

Some disused quarries have become very important habitats for wildlife — they are also useful places for learning about geology.

EXAMPLES

Quarrying in progress

Quarrying causes a Conflict of Land Use

Granite, limestone and chalk are all quarried, which produces conflicts between the quarrying companies, locals and the tourist industry. Learn both sides of the argument because examiners love this conflict stuff.

FACT

Nowadays it's very hard to get permission to start or extend a quarry, especially in a tourist area.

Good Things about Quarries	Bad Things about Quarries
Quarries provide building materials, e.g. cement, and lime (used in fertilisers). They also provide road & rail materials, e.g. sand / gravel, limestone chippings.	They're noisy, dusty eyesores which put people off coming to the area.
They provide employment at the quarry and associated businesses like road building, haulage, catering, etc.	They increase the traffic (big, slow, smelly trucks).
When the quarrying has stopped they can be used as lakes for wildlife reserves and sporting uses.	When the quarrying has stopped they're often used as landfill sites which can be bad for the environment.

Limestone Quarrying in Derbyshire causes Conflict

Quarrying is needed to keep up with the demand for raw materials, but it causes conflicts in the area.

UK LOCATION

Opportunities from quarrying:
- Jobs are created for local people — about 10% of Derbyshire's male employment is in mining and quarrying.

- Limestone is an important building material and can be used to make fertiliser and cement. It is therefore a very important requirement of other industries, e.g. the building trade, farming, road construction.

- The excess stone extracted from around Ladybower reservoir is being used to support the dam and therefore preserve the reservoir.

- The quarry can later be landscaped to make an attractive wildlife area.

Conflicts over quarrying:
- Quarrying is happening in the Peak District National Park, creating an ugly grey scar on the beautiful landscape, and making lots of dust and pollution.

- Tourists may decide not to visit the area due to the ugly quarry.

- Local people don't like the huge, noisy polluting lorries.

- National park officers want quarrying stopped to preserve the natural landscape and ecosystems.

Tropical Rainforests

Section Four
People & the Environment

Tropical rainforests are a beautiful but vulnerable environment. If they continue to be cleared for commercial reasons, they will one day disappear forever.

Equatorial Climates have Tropical Rainforests — TRFs

A tropical rainforest (TRF) has hot, humid, growing conditions with many different species per unit area — it has two tree layers and a sparse undergrowth layer.

Dominant plants are tall trees like mahogany — umbrella-shaped, with branches near their crowns where most light reaches them. These emergent trees stick out above the others.

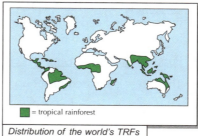
■ = tropical rainforest
Distribution of the world's TRFs

Below the emergent trees is the canopy layer, a dense collection of trees, home to birds and monkeys, which lets through little light. Below the canopy layer are smaller trees and plants such as orchids, but little undergrowth due to the lack of light. Animals like frogs and tapirs live on the forest floor.

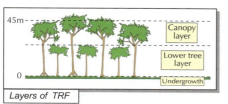
Layers of TRF

Plants adapt to the heavy rainfall with thick, waxy drip-tip leaves which water runs off. Trees have buttress roots to support their tall trunks. Equatorial climate areas have no definite seasons — so two neighbouring plants can be fruiting and flowering at the same time.

EXAMPLES

Tropical rainforests
South America e.g. Brazil (Amazon Basin)
Central Africa e.g. Cameroon
South East Asia e.g. Borneo

The TRF has a Nutrient Cycle

The frequent heavy rainfall and constant high temperatures are ideal conditions for vegetation growth.

TRF soils are called latosols. The soil is enriched by rotting leaves and dead animals. It has a very fertile top layer. The trees in the TRF have very wide shallow roots to take advantage of the nutrients in the top layer of the soil.

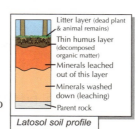
Latosol soil profile

The TRF is very Vulnerable to Change

The balance of plant and animal life in the TRF is very delicate and extremely vulnerable to change. If vegetation is removed, the soil quickly becomes infertile. This is because there will be no more fallen leaves to enrich the top layer of soil.

There will also be fewer leaves and branches to intercept rainwater, meaning that more water will reach the ground. This causes leaching, which is when the rain removes the minerals and nutrients from the soil's top layer, and soil erosion. TRFs are cleared for a number of reasons:

- TRF trees are mainly hardwoods so they are very valuable. In many places the logging industry has cleared large areas of TRF.

- In order to set up large cattle ranches, farmers have chopped down vast areas of TRF. The fragile and unprotected soil is quickly eroded by overgrazing by cattle, and the rain and becomes infertile.

- To provide hydro-electric power for industries like mining and paper mills, large dams have been built. The dams created large reservoirs that have destroyed animals and plants by ruining their natural habitat.

Section Four
People & the Environment

Deforestation and Conservation

The removal of trees on a large scale is called deforestation.
Deforestation is a problem in many TRFs, like the Amazon rainforest in Brazil.

Trees in Brazil are Disappearing for *Five* Reasons

- Logging for export to MEDCs — trees should be replanted so the industry can keep selling them long-term, but many LEDCs want to make money today and don't plant for the future.

- Population is increasing — settlement and road-building in the TRF is needed.

- The forest is cleared to set up cattle ranches, which quickly make land useless.

- Mineral extraction helps Brazil pay foreign debts — Carajas in Brazil is the world's largest iron reserve.

- HEP development has meant that large areas of land have been flooded.

EXAMPLE

Deforestation in Brazil

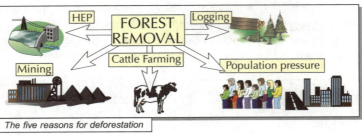

The five reasons for deforestation

There are Two Sides to the Deforestation Debate

For Conservation

- Agricultural development is pointless — soils robbed of TRF lose fertility, so farming can't continue after three or four years.

- Medicinal products could be destroyed before they're discovered — medicines have been found in TRFs before.

- Heritage value means preserving this ecosystem for future generations — there are many native tribes whose way of life is being destroyed.

- Global warming is reduced by trees using carbon dioxide in photosynthesis — so removing the forest means more global warming.

- Forest removal lowers evapotranspiration — and rainfall — altering the climate.

For Deforestation

- Poor countries need to use their resources to help their people.

- Many MEDCs destroyed their own forests when developing — the UK did (although not so fast) — so they shouldn't have one rule for themselves and one for LEDCs who need to develop.

- Nearly 75% of world carbon dioxide emissions comes from MEDCs — why should LEDCs have to change policy first?

- If LEDCs are removing forest to earn money to pay MEDCs, then MEDCs could lower interest or cancel debts if they're so worried about deforestation.

- MEDCs are buying the products of these areas — so why should LEDCs stop?

EXAMPLES

Forest removal lowers evapotranspiration and rainfall — altering the climate:
Ethiopia was 40% forest in the early 1900s, but is now only 2%. This has increased drought, as rainfall has been reduced.

EXAM TIP

Remember — no matter what your own opinion is, you'll only get top marks in the exam if you know both sides of the argument.

Malaysia sets an example to other countries — it exports one third of the world's hardwoods and the government has strict controls.
Trees have to be a certain age and height before they're felled and companies must replant as many trees as they remove.

Sustainable Development in Forests

Section Four
People & the Environment

Deforestation has to become sustainable, or there'll soon be no forest left.

The World's Forests are Disappearing Fast

Forests all over the world are being destroyed for wood, redevelopment, fossil fuels, and farming. Twelve million hectares of the world's forests disappear every year. That's an area half the size of the UK lost every year and it's getting worse.

This has been known for a long time. The problem is getting people to change their use of forests when it means making less money in the short-term.

FACT

1 hectare = 10 000 m^2

The Five Big Sustainable Forestry Techniques

Cabling — Most forestry is done by clear cutting, which is just ploughing into the forest and cutting down lots of trees you don't want to get to the ones you do. Cabling, or heli-logging, is where you air-lift trees out by helicopter, which reduces the amount of needless destruction.

Cabling

Replanting — Replacing trees that are cut down. More and more laws insist that logging companies do this nowadays. It's important that the right kinds of trees are planted — planting rubber trees instead of a whole load of different rainforest species isn't good enough.

Zoning — Identifying areas (or zones) for different uses. Different areas are set aside for things like tourism, forestry and mining. Some zones are set up as national parks to protect the forest ecosystem.

Trucks cause damage

Selective logging — A method used by small, environmentally sound logging businesses. Only selected trees are chopped — most are left standing. The best trees are left standing to maintain a strong gene pool. The least intrusive form is 'horse logging' — dragging felled trees out of the forest using horses not trucks.

Natural regeneration — This means leaving areas of forest to recover naturally before removing trees again.

FACT

Deforestation has been happening for many centuries. When the Greek and Roman civilisations developed, many natural forests were cleared to make space for farming and settlement. Little natural woodland still exists today, but has been replaced by scrub instead.

EXAMPLES

Small scale projects: The Body Shop buying groundnut oil from small scale projects run by locals.

Resource conservation: Making cars and power stations more efficient so you use less fuel.

Resource substitution: Using recyclable aluminium instead of steel for making cans, or using wind power instead of coal.

There's a Three Pronged Attack on Bad Forestry

Promoting sustainable use of the forests:
- Creating a demand for sustainable products. Clearly labelling products from 'sustainably managed forests'.
- Encouraging small scale projects.
- Encouraging ecotourism by advertising and education.

Discouraging bad practice:
- Banning wood from forests that are managed non-sustainably.
- Preventing illegal logging and enforcing protected areas.
- Putting pressure on businesses to only buy from sustainable forests.

Saving Forests

Reducing the need for large scale deforestation:
- Debt-for-nature swaps — some of the countries' debt can be bought back by governments or conservation organisations in return for conservation projects.

Sustainable Use of Resources Needs Good Stewardship

- Resource conservation — Using resources carefully to slow their consumption.
- Resource substitution — Changing resources for more sustainable ones.
- Pollution control — Limiting pollution to reduce global warming and acid rain.
- Recycling — Reducing waste produced and conserving resources.

KEY TERM

Stewardship means using resources responsibly so some are left and so damage caused is minimal.

Section Four — People & the Environment

National Parks

National parks have been set up in the UK to protect different wild environments and maintain them in their natural state.

National Parks are Protected Areas

There are 12 national parks, mostly situated away from large population centres. The South Downs and the New Forest are waiting to be confirmed as national parks.

They are areas of outstanding natural beauty, including large areas of mountain and moorland — and they are protected by law for the enjoyment of all members of the public.

Much of the land is privately owned.

They contain many permanent settlements like villages.

They are looked after by the National Parks Authority (NPA).

UK map showing national parks

The NPA has Three Jobs

- The NPA protects the environment.
- It promotes the enjoyment and understanding of the parks.
- It looks after the interests of the residents.

Many people come to the parks for outdoor activities and to enjoy their peace and natural beauty — the motorway network allows easy access.

EXAMPLES

Industry destroying the ethos of the park: Limestone quarrying in the Peak District provides jobs yet it destroys the landscape that people come to see.

Honeypot area: Bowness-on-Windermere in the Lake District.

'Park and ride' scheme: Peak District national park.

The Use of the Parks Causes Conflict

- Planning regulations are very strict, and development is strictly controlled.
- Some industries in the parks destroy the ethos of the park.
- Visitors and tourists provide jobs and income for residents, but cause traffic congestion, pollution, litter and footpath erosion.
- Visitors can cause damage to farmland and animals, destroying farmers' livelihoods.

Visitors can damage farmers' land

Honeypot areas are the popular spots that become so overused by tourists that they start to change (e.g. supermarkets and hotels are built to cater for the visitors) and eventually lose the character that made them special.

KEY POINT

The main issue here is finding a balance between encouraging more visitors and tourists, and stopping them from destroying a protected environment.

Conflicts can be Resolved — Slowly

The NPA tries to resolve conflicts through public enquiries.

Planning and development restrictions can control what goes on — e.g. 'park and ride' schemes can be used to reduce the numbers of vehicles to parts of a park.

Case Study

**Section Four
People & the Environment**

You need to know an example of the conflicts and solutions to conflict in a particular National Park.

Case Study: <u>Conflicts</u> in <u>Dartmoor</u> National Park

Around 8 million people visit <u>Dartmoor</u> each year. People visit Dartmoor to admire the <u>scenery</u>, walk, mountain bike or use the reservoirs for water sports. When people visit Dartmoor, they also stay in hotels, eat in restaurants and use local shops. This brings a lot of <u>money</u> to the area, so tourism is <u>encouraged</u>. However, there are <u>conflicts of interest</u> on Dartmoor.

UK LOCATION

Dartmoor

Conflicts on Dartmoor include:

- There is an <u>army camp</u> in the northern part of Dartmoor. At certain times the army practises firing live ammunition and if tourists are not careful they can find themselves in <u>danger</u> of injury.

The army use Dartmoor for training

- China clay is <u>mined</u> on the southwest border of Dartmoor. This produces big ugly <u>waste tips</u> which stand out against the landscape and put off tourists.

- Farmers are <u>unhappy</u> when tourists walking dogs disturb their sheep.

- High numbers of <u>tourist vehicles</u> have put a great strain on narrow local roads.

Tourists drop litter and erode footpaths

- Certain areas ('<u>honeypot</u>' sites), such as the banks of the river Dart, attract more visitors than other areas. This means they experience traffic congestion, littering and footpath erosion.

- Recreational activities like mountain biking, water sports and hiking have put pressure on <u>natural resources</u>.

There are some attempts to <u>solve</u> the <u>conflicts</u>

- Clearly marked <u>walking trails</u> are created to try and keep tourists away from <u>farm animals</u>, and to prevent them from trampling on and <u>ruining farmland</u>. Some parts of the moor have been made <u>out of bounds</u> to tourists.

- The army puts up <u>warning signs</u> to prevent tourists straying into firing ranges.

- The National Parks Authority (NPA) has introduced <u>car parks</u> and <u>tourist information centres</u> in an attempt to encourage tourists to use these areas and so keep away from areas unable to cope with large numbers. Some roads have been restricted to <u>local-use</u> only.

- The NPA has tried to encourage tourists to visit areas other than the 'honeypot' sites to try and reduce the <u>pressure</u> on those sites.

- More <u>tourist facilities</u> have been introduced to reduce the strain placed on some areas. Attractions such as the High Moorland Visitor Centre and the Dartmoor Wildlife Centre help to take pressure of the Park's natural resources.

Section Four — People & the Environment

Pollution

Pollution is any damage caused to the environment — whether it's damage to air, water or land.

Pollution is a Global Problem

Pollution is found worldwide. Pollution created in one part of the world can affect other areas. Almost any human activity can cause pollution — industry, transport and agriculture, for example. Ugly buildings, tips and quarries cause visual pollution, and aircraft cause noise pollution.

> **EXAMPLES**
> Radioactive fallout from the Chernobyl disaster in the Ukraine affected north-west England.

There are Four Common Types of Pollution

Air pollution is caused by burning fossil fuels for industrial, domestic and transport use — giving off gases like sulphur dioxide and carbon monoxide in smoke. Agricultural chemicals also get into the air.

Air pollution

River and sea pollution

River pollution is caused by untreated industrial waste and dirty water. Fertilisers and pesticides from agriculture also get washed into water courses. Hot water from power stations causes thermal pollution.

Sea pollution is mainly caused by dirty water from industry, oil slicks and spills, and untreated human sewage. Household waste is sometimes dumped in the sea.

Land pollution is caused by agricultural chemicals, waste material from mines and quarries, scrap, industrial waste and household waste.

Pollution has Serious Harmful Effects

> **EXAMPLES**
>
> **Effects of water pollution:**
> Untreated sewage spreads diseases like cholera.
>
> **Effects of pollutants in the food chain:**
> People died in Minamata Bay, Japan, eating fish contaminated by industrial mercury waste.
>
> **Effects of industrial pollution:**
> Asbestos (used as an insulator) gives off dust which causes cancer. The use of asbestos in buildings is now strictly controlled.

- Air pollution causes acid rain, increases the greenhouse effect (see p.72), and is linked to illnesses like asthma.

- Water pollution can poison the water supply and destroy river habitats. Fertilisers and untreated sewage cause algae to grow much faster. The algae use up oxygen which causes fish and other organisms to die. Thermal pollution interferes with the natural balance in water systems and damages fish life. Oil spillages damage sea life, bird life and plant life.

- Land pollution can kill wildlife — e.g. insecticides kill insects and the animals that eat them.

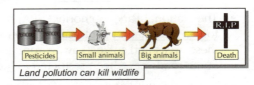
Land pollution can kill wildlife

- Many pollutants stay around for years because they get into animal and human food chains.

- Some chemical waste products from industry are toxic, which is harmful to humans and wildlife.

- Radioactive waste from nuclear power is indestructible. High level wastes cause cancer and genetic defects in most life forms.

Reducing pollution is an expensive business. It means making sacrifices, like increased electricity bills for greener power stations and limited car use to cut exhaust emissions — some people don't want the hassle.

Acid Rain

**Section Four
People & the Environment**

Acid rain is basically rain which has a higher than normal acid level (i.e. a low pH).

Acid Rain comes from Burning Fossil Fuels

Burning coal, oil and natural gas in power stations gives off sulphur dioxide gas.
Burning petrol and oil in vehicle engines gives off nitrogen oxides as gases.

These gases mix with water vapour and rain water in the atmosphere, producing weak solutions of sulphuric and nitric acids — which fall as acid rain.

The formation of acid rain

Acid Rain can Travel Long Distances

Often acid rain doesn't fall where the gases are produced — high chimneys disperse the gases and winds blow them great distances before they dissolve and fall to Earth as rain.

FACT

Acid rain travels. Gases produced in England can result in acid rain in Scotland and Scandinavia.

Acid Rain Damages Nature and Buildings

- Leaves and tree roots can die from the poison in the rain.
- High acid levels make rivers and lakes unsuitable for fish.
- Acid rain increases 'leaching', which removes nutrients from soils. This causes crop yields to decrease.
- Some nutrients which get into rivers and lakes can kill plant and animal life.
- Acid rain dissolves the stonework and mortar of buildings.

Lime can reduce the effects of acid rain when added to rivers, lakes and soils by neutralising acids — but it's expensive and doesn't always work.

Acid rain affects trees, rivers and buildings

EXAMPLES

Some problems caused by acid rain:
- Forests in Germany and Scandinavia have been destroyed.
- Upland pastures in Scotland have become infertile.
- York Minster has a lot of crumbling stonework.

Acid Rain Production can be Reduced

- Sulphur dioxide can be removed from power station chimneys but this process is expensive.
- Less sulphur dioxide will be produced if the demand for electricity is reduced, or if the electricity is generated using other production methods, e.g. HEP (see p.59 and p.60).
- Fitting catalytic converters to vehicle exhausts removes the nitrogen oxides.
- Limiting the number of road vehicles and increasing public transport would cut down on exhaust gas emissions.

International Cooperation is Very Important

It's crucial that countries work together and help each other.
All the countries of the world are part of a global community.

It's vital that governments around the world realise that their actions affect the global climate as well as their own local climate.

Section Four: People & the Environment

Global Warming

The average global temperature has risen by over ½ °C in the last hundred years — and the years since 1980 have been the hottest on record.

Global Warming is caused by Increased Fossil Fuel Use

Since the Industrial Revolution, people have needed more energy for work and in the home — this has come from burning more fossil fuels, particularly coal and oil.

This burning releases more carbon dioxide and methane into the atmosphere — these increase what's known as the 'greenhouse effect'.

EXAMPLES
Don't worry about all the complex science behind global warming. All you need to know are the main principles of how global warming happens and the consequences of increasing temperatures.

The Earth is like a Giant Greenhouse

Energy from the Sun passes through the atmosphere as light and warms up the Earth. When the energy is radiated and reflected back off the surface as heat, it is trapped by the atmosphere and can't get back out into space — this is like how a greenhouse keeps the heat inside. Increasing the greenhouse gases, e.g. carbon dioxide, increases the greenhouse effect, which means the Earth gets hotter.

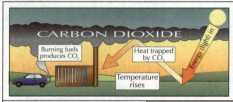
The greenhouse effect in action

The World's Climates could Change

- Higher temperatures mean that ice-sheets and glaciers are beginning to melt and low lying areas of the world are under threat of flooding.
- Droughts, floods and storms could get more severe, widespread and common.
- The northern hemisphere wheat belt could get more arid and less productive.
- Tundra in Arctic areas could get warmer and support crop growth.
- The Sahara desert could spread north into southern Europe.
- The North Atlantic drift (a major ocean current) could be altered, causing Britain to get much colder.

FACT
Sea levels have risen by 0.25m in the last 100 years. In 100 years, they will probably rise another 0.5m.

Global Warming needs to be Managed

To reduce global warming as much as possible, people should be encouraged to avoid wasting electricity. This reduces the amount of fossil fuels burned so less carbon dioxide is released into the atmosphere. Where possible, governments should develop renewable energy sources (see p.59).

It is important to recycle waste products so less methane is released into the atmosphere by landfill sites. People should also walk, cycle and use public transport more often. This reduces the level of carbon dioxide produced by cars. 'Local Agenda 21' sets out guidelines to help communities reduce their emissions.

EXAMPLES
Areas at risk of flooding if sea levels continue to rise include parts of south-east England, and the Nile and Ganges deltas. Many of the world's major cities, like London and New York, are also under threat.

There's Conflict Over Reducing Greenhouse Gases

To prevent further global warming, greenhouse gas emissions need to be reduced. But some countries disagree over whether to do this for different reasons:

- Many countries use fossil fuels but want to reduce gas emissions.
- India and other LEDCs don't want to reduce gas emissions because their development would slow down.
- Oil states don't want to because their revenues from oil sales would decrease.
- The USA is reluctant to because it doesn't want a fall in living standards.

Case Study

**Section Four
People & the Environment**

The following case study is about what has caused the Mediterranean Sea to become polluted, what effects pollution has had, and how the authorities are trying to repair the damage done.

Case Study: Pollution in the Mediterranean Basin

There are Different Causes of the Pollution in the Mediterranean:

- The Mediterranean is almost totally surrounded by land which means it isn't affected by tides. So the water isn't cleaned naturally by tides and pollutants tend to be trapped in the basin.
- The region has a hot climate which means there is high evaporation. This creates a high concentration of pollutants in the sea.
- 90% of the sewage produced by those living around the Mediterranean enters the sea untreated.
- The Mediterranean is a popular summer destination for tourists. There are many tourist developments on the coast that create high levels of pollution.

Cleaning a beach after an oil spillage

- Industrialisation around the Mediterranean means there are oil refineries, steel works and chemical plants that are dumping waste into the sea.
- There have been a number of oil spillages that have affected the region.
- Many of the rivers that enter the Mediterranean (e.g. the Rhône, from France) are polluted themselves.

Pollution has Affected Tourism and Sea Life

Parts of the sea are now so polluted that they are dangerous for people to swim in. Areas that used to be very popular with tourists are less popular because of pollution.

Fish and other sea life are suffering because of the pollution. Some species of fish have actually disappeared altogether. Some of the fish and shellfish caught in the sea are not fit to eat because pollutants have contaminated them.

Pollution affects tourism

Pollution can be Reduced

Eighteen countries met and signed the 'Blue Plan' in 1979. The aim of the plan was to improve the Mediterranean environment by reducing pollution.

All the countries agreed to end chemical dumping, to work together to prevent oil spillages and to build new sewage treatment plants on the coast. These new strategies reduce pollution and are more sustainable.

The Blue Plan has reduced pollution in a lot of the Mediterranean. Unfortunately it is still a problem in places, especially around many poorer countries, such as Greece, that tend to be more concerned with creating new industries than with protecting the environment.

Section Four
People & the Environment

Revision Summary

There's a lot to get sorted in this section about the world's most beautiful and diverse places... and how humans are gradually destroying them. There are loads of tricky words and phrases — so have a go at these questions and find out how many you know. If you get stuck or have problems then look back over the section until it's all clear.

Human Use of the Environment and Conflicts

1) List four things that might be quarried.
2) Which groups of people might conflict over quarries?
3) List three good things about quarries.
4) List three bad things about quarries.
5) Write a mini-essay to contrast the opportunities and conflicts surrounding quarrying in Derbyshire.
6) In what type of climate are tropical rainforests found?
7) Name the two tree layers in a TRF and describe the vegetation of each.
8) Why is there little undergrowth in a TRF?
9) Name the type of soil found in TRFs. How have trees adapted to get the most nutrients out of this type of soil?
10) Name three places with TRFs.
11) What is leaching and how is it caused?
12) Give three reasons why TRFs have been cleared.
13) List five reasons for deforestation in Brazil.
14) Write a mini-essay to discuss the two sides of the deforestation debate.
15) Describe the strict controls on forestry in Malaysia.
16) What are cabling and zoning? How are they sustainable?
17) Name three other sustainable forestry techniques.
18) Write a mini-essay on how to save forests. (There are three main ways.)
19) Define the term 'stewardship'.
20) List five national parks in the UK.
21) Why might tourists visit a national park?
22) Give the three main tasks of the National Park Authority.
23) What problems do tourists cause for national parks?
24) What is a honeypot area? Give an example.
25) Give one way in which the NPA tries to resolve conflicts.
26) Why do so many people visit Dartmoor each year?
27) Give three conflicts of interest on Dartmoor.
28) Give four ways people are trying to resolve these conflicts.

EXAM TIP

Conflict is a common theme in geography. Different groups of people have different interests, and one of the things geography looks at is how best to solve these conflicts — it's all to do with compromise. So make sure you're clued up about different groups' interests, because you nearly always have to mention both sides to a debate in the exam.

Revision Summary

Section Four
People & the Environment

There's a lot of stuff in here — pollution, acid rain, global warming. They seem like separate topics, but they're not — they're all about how humans affect the environment by using natural resources.

Pollution

1) Explain with an example why pollution is considered to be a global problem.
2) What are the major causes of: a) air pollution; b) river pollution?
3) Suggest two ways in which air pollution could be reduced.
4) Explain why pollutants like mercury and radioactive waste are so dangerous.
5) Why might a reduction in pollution prove to be unpopular?
6) Explain how acid rain is caused.
7) Why doesn't acid rain always fall in the area where it is produced?
8) List three of the damaging effects of acid rain.
9) What are the drawbacks of using lime to combat acid rain?
10) Give three ways in which the production of acid rain can be reduced.
11) Give a named example of a problem caused by acid rain.
12) What evidence is there that global warming is taking place?
13) What causes the greenhouse effect?
    Use a diagram to show how this works.
14) Describe how global warming could cause low areas to flood.
15) Give three possible ways in which the world's climate could change.
16) What can be done to manage global warming?
17) Explain why LEDCs, oil states and the USA are reluctant to reduce greenhouse gas emissions.
18) How has the Mediterranean being surrounded by land affected pollution?
19) Give three other causes of pollution in the Mediterranean.
20) How has pollution in the Mediterranean affected a) tourism; b) sea life?
21) What is the 'Blue Plan'? When was it introduced?
    Describe one of its successes and one of its failures.

EXAM TIP

These revision summaries are a really important part of your revision so don't skip them. When you can answer all of the questions on a section, then you're halfway there to being totally prepared for the exam.

Section Five
Geographical Skills

Ordnance Survey Maps

These two pages have everything you need to know about Ordnance Survey maps for the exam — <u>essential</u> if you want to get some easy marks.

Know your <u>Compass Points</u>

You've got to know the compass — for giving <u>directions</u>, saying which way a <u>river's flowing</u>, or knowing what they mean if they say 'look at the river in the <u>NW</u> of the map'. Read it <u>out loud</u> to yourself, going <u>clockwise</u>.

The four main compass points

Use a <u>Ruler</u> to Measure <u>Straight Distances</u>

EXAM TIP
Using a ruler is the only way to get distances that are accurate — there's no point just trying to guess.

To work out the <u>distance</u> between two features use a <u>ruler</u> to measure in cm and then <u>compare</u> it to the scale to work out the distance in km.

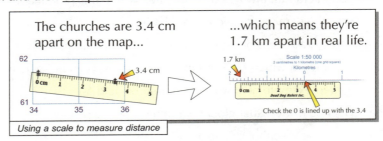

Using a scale to measure distance

Use <u>String</u> to Measure <u>Winding Distances</u>

To work out the distance between points along a bendy route (e.g. to find the length of a twisty road or river) lay a <u>piece of string</u> along the route, following all the <u>curves</u>. You can then <u>compare</u> the length of the string with the scale to work out the distance, just like using a ruler for straight distances.

<u>Grid References</u> Tell you Where Something is

EXAM TIP
If you're asked to give a grid reference in the <u>exam</u>, always check whether they want a <u>four</u>-figure or a <u>six</u>-figure one.

There are two kinds of grid reference: four figure grid references and six figure grid references.

Here's how to work out both, for the Post Office on this map.

Four-Figure Grid References:

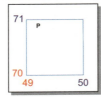

Find the square you want.
Find the <u>Eastings</u> (across) value for the <u>left</u> side of the square (<u>49</u>).
Find the <u>Northings</u> (up) value for the <u>bottom</u> of the square (<u>70</u>).
Write the numbers together. The grid reference is <u>4970</u>.

Six-Figure Grid References:

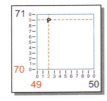

Start by working out the <u>basic</u> Eastings and Northings as above.
Then imagine the square's divided into <u>tenths</u>.
Divide it by <u>eye</u> — or even better use your <u>ruler</u>.
The Eastings value is now <u>492</u> (49 and 2 "tenths")
and the Northings is <u>709</u> (70 and 9 "tenths").
The six-figure reference is <u>492709</u>.

* © Crown copyright, License no. 100034841

Ordnance Survey Maps

**Section Five
Geographical Skills**

This page contains more things you need to know about using OS maps.

Relief is Shown by *Contours* and *Spot Heights*

Contours are those orange lines on Ordnance Survey maps. They're imaginary lines joining points of equal height above sea-level.

If a map has lots of contour lines on it, it's a hilly or mountainous area. If there are only a few contour lines, it'll be flat, and usually low-lying.

The steeper the slope is, the closer the contours get.
The flatter it is, the more spaced out they are. Look at these examples:

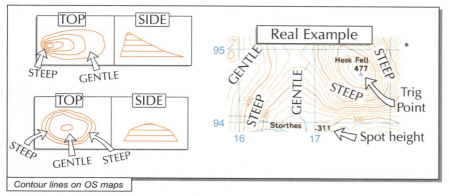

Contour lines on OS maps

A spot height is a dot giving the height of a particular place.
A trigonometrical point (trig point) is a blue triangle plus a height value, showing the highest point in an area (in metres).

EXAM TIP

Contours are a kind of isoline — there's more stuff about understanding them and drawing them on page 83.

EXAM TIP

Contours can give you ideas about the land use of an area. Hilly areas are often recreational places and might be used for grazing animals. Flatter areas are more likely to have settlements or be used for growing crops.

Sketching Maps — do it *Carefully*

In the exam, they can give you a printed map and tell you to copy part of it onto an empty grid. Pretty straightforward, but you've got to get it right.

Make sure you read what bit they want you to draw out, and double check. It might be only part of a lake or a wood, or only one of the roads.

EXAMPLE: *Q: Sketch the lake and the main roads and rivers on this map.*

 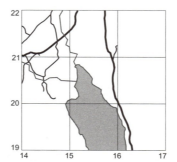

- Get the right shapes in the right place in the squares.
- It's a good idea to measure a few of the important points to help you — if you copy a few things over really accurately then filling in the other bits will be easier.
- Get the widths of the roads right.
- Draw your sketch in pencil so you can rub it out if it's wrong.

Drawing sketch maps

EXAM TIP

If you're asked to make a sketch map in the exam, see if you can lay the grid over the map — then you can trace bits of it.

* © Crown copyright, License no. 100034841

Section Five
Geographical Skills

Human Geography — Plans and Photos

Plans, like maps, show places from above.
And like maps, there are a few <u>tricks</u> you need to learn.

Look at the Shapes when you Compare <u>Plans</u> and <u>Photos</u>

The simplest question they could ask you is something like *"Name the place labelled A on the photo"*. Names are on the <u>plan</u>, so you've got to work out how the photo <u>matches</u> the plan.

Look for the main <u>features</u> on the <u>photo</u> and find them on the <u>plan</u> — things with an interesting <u>shape</u> like a <u>lake</u>, or big <u>roads</u> and <u>railways</u>.

EXAMPLE ONE:

> Q: Name the place labelled A on the photo.
>
> A: By the <u>shape</u> of the land, it's either got to be <u>Hope Point</u> or <u>Dead Dog Point</u>.
>
> There isn't a <u>road</u> or <u>building</u> at point A, so it <u>can't</u> be Dead Dog Point — it <u>must</u> be <u>Hope Point</u>.

 Plan of St. James Harbour, 1984

 Photograph of St. James Harbour, 1986

Comparing photographs and plans

EXAM TIP

If you're asked to look at plans and photos in the exam, be aware that they might not be the <u>same way up</u>. Spend a bit of time working out which way up they need to be so you don't get too confused.

The other type of question is when they ask <u>what's changed</u> between the photo and the plan and <u>why</u>. Look at the shapes to find <u>what's</u> changed, then look at what it's being <u>used for now</u> (check the dates).

EXAMPLE TWO:

> Q: Where has land been reclaimed from the sea? Suggest why.
>
> A: By the <u>shape</u> of the land, it's got to be <u>Baldy Bay</u> — the sea's further from that building now. It's being used as a car park, so they must have needed more parking.

A typical question about change over time

Plans of <u>Towns</u> and <u>Aerial Photos</u> — Look at the Buildings

When you get a <u>plan</u> in the exam, start by looking at the <u>types of buildings</u> and what's <u>around</u> them.

<u>Small</u> buildings are probably <u>houses</u> or <u>shops</u>.
<u>Bigger</u> buildings are probably <u>factories</u> or <u>schools</u>.

Work out what <u>kind of area</u> it is — lots of <u>car parks</u> and <u>shops</u> mean it's a <u>CBD</u>, <u>houses</u> with <u>gardens</u> mean a <u>residential area</u>, a <u>group of houses</u> surrounded by <u>fields</u> means a <u>village</u>.
Always read the <u>labels</u> — they can give you a lot of easy clues.

EXAM TIP

If you get an <u>aerial photo</u> instead of a plan, treat it in exactly the same way — look for types of buildings and what kind of area it is. You can see the cars and trees which helps, but there won't be any labels.

EXAMPLE:

> This area has <u>houses</u> with front and back <u>gardens</u>, a <u>park</u>, a <u>school</u> and a <u>college</u>. So it's a <u>residential area</u> — you can tell it's <u>not</u> a CBD and <u>not</u> dense inner-city housing.

Describing Maps and Charts

Section Five
Geographical Skills

Describing distributions and photos can seem tricky, but it's pretty easy once you've got the hang of it.

Distribution on Maps — Keep it Simple
This is an example of the type of question you might get:

> Q: Use the map to describe the distribution of areas with a population density of less than 10 persons per km².
>
> Questions like this aren't easy — you can see where those pale yellow patches are, but putting it into words seems silly. Don't panic — just write down a description of where things are.
>
> A: The areas with a population density less than 10 persons per km² are distributed in the north of Scotland, the north and south-west of England, and northern Wales.

A typical question about distribution on maps

EXAM TIP

Describe places using the compass points — its the easiest way to make sure the examiner knows which area you're talking about.

```
      North
West        East
      South
```

Another worked example:

> Q: Use the maps to describe the distribution of National Parks in Spondovia.
>
> They've given you two maps, which means they want you to look at them both. Look at the first map and say where the blobs are, then look at the second map and say if there's any link or not:
>
> A: The National Parks are distributed in the south-west and north-east of Spondovia. They are all located in mountainous areas.

A typical question describing distributions

Describing Photos — Stick to What They Ask You For
Double-check what the question's asking. Don't tell them everything if they only want what you can see from the photo — you won't get the marks. Look at these two examples for this photo:

> The photo shows a 'honeypot site'.
> List the factors that attract tourists to honeypot locations.
> This is asking you to tell them everything you know.
>
> The photo shows a 'honeypot site'.
> List three factors that would attract tourists to this location.
> This is asking you to list only the things you can see in this photo.

If they're asking you what you can see in the photo, then don't over-complicate things — stick to what you can see in the photo. For example, if they asked how people are affecting erosion of cliffs in this photo, then the answer is by walking on them (the footpath), not the cars causing acid rain or something.

When you get a photo, look for physical geography clues (what the land's like), e.g. coastal features and river features, and the human geography stuff (what the land is used for) e.g. the types of buildings, if there are any car parks, if there are roads or paths, etc.

Use your head — for example if it looks nice and there's a car park, you can guess there'll be tourism.

Typical questions about describing photographs

EXAM TIP

Remember to double-check whether they want you to describe what you can see in the photo or to talk about something in a wider sense.

KEY TERM

A honeypot site is a recreational area which attracts a very large number of visitors to a relatively small space.

Section Five
Geographical Skills

Types of Graphs and Charts

Two things you need to be able to do here. Number one: know how to <u>read</u> all of the types of graphs. Number two: know how to <u>fill in</u> all of the types of graphs. It's exactly what you have to do in the <u>exam</u>.

Bar Charts — Draw the Bars *Straight* and *Neat*

How to Read Bar Charts
Read along the <u>bottom</u> to find the <u>bar</u> you want.
Read from the <u>top</u> of the bar across to the <u>scale</u>, and read off the number.

EXAMPLE:

Q: *How many tonnes of oil does Russia produce per year?*

A: Go up the Russia bar, read across, and it's about 620 on the scale — but the scale's in thousands of tonnes, so the answer is <u>620 000 tonnes</u>.

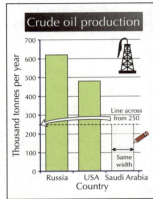

Crude oil production

How to Fill in Bar Charts
First find the number you want on the <u>vertical scale</u>.
With a <u>ruler</u>, trace a line across and draw in a bar of the <u>right size</u>.

EXAMPLE:

Q: *Complete the graph to show that Saudi Arabia produces 250 thousand tonnes of crude oil per year.*

A: Find 250 on the scale, trace a line across, then draw the bar in, the <u>same width</u> as the others.

EXAM TIP

When you're filling in graphs use a <u>ruler</u> or it'll look scruffy and you'll lose marks.

Line Graphs — the Points are Joined by *Lines*

How to Read Line Graphs
Read along the <u>bottom</u> to find the number you want.
Read up to the line you want, then read across to the <u>vertical scale</u>.

EXAMPLE:

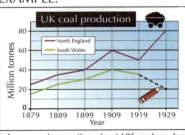

Q: *How much coal did the north of England produce in 1919?*

A: Find 1919, go up to the purple line, read across, and it's 50 on the scale. The scale's in millions of tonnes, so the answer is <u>50 million tonnes</u>.

An example question about UK coal production

EXAM TIP

Make sure you look at <u>scales</u> when you're answering questions that involve graphs. You need to know what units are being used. Also check where the scale starts — numbers on the axes don't always start at 0.

How to Fill in Line Graphs
Find the value you want on the <u>bottom scale</u>.
Go up to get the right value on the <u>vertical scale</u>.
<u>Double-check</u> you're still at the right value from the <u>bottom</u>, then make a <u>mark</u>.
Using a <u>ruler</u>, join the mark to the line.

EXAMPLE:

Q: *Complete the graph to show that South Wales produced 20 million tonnes of coal in 1929.*

A: Find 1929 on the bottom, then go up to 20 million tonnes and make a mark, then join it to the green line <u>with a ruler</u>.

Types of Graphs and Charts

**Section Five
Geographical Skills**

Pie charts and triangular graphs are both ways of showing <u>percentages</u>.

Pie Charts Show Percentages

How to Read Pie Charts

Read numbers off a <u>pie chart with a scale</u> like this:

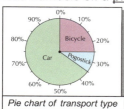
Pie chart of transport type

To work out the % for a wedge, write down where it <u>starts</u> and <u>ends</u>, then <u>subtract</u>.

For example, the '<u>Car</u>' wedge goes from 35% to 100%: 100 − 35 = <u>65%</u>

They can ask you to <u>estimate</u> the percentage on a pie chart <u>without a scale</u>, but they'll only give you <u>easy</u> ones:

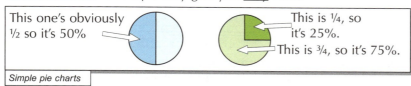
Simple pie charts

How to Fill In Pie Charts

With a <u>ruler</u>, draw lines from the <u>centre</u> to <u>0%</u>, and to the number on the <u>outside</u> that you want. Here's how you'd do <u>45%</u>:

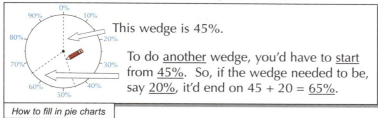
How to fill in pie charts

This wedge is 45%.

To do <u>another</u> wedge, you'd have to <u>start</u> from <u>45%</u>. So, if the wedge needed to be, say <u>20%</u>, it'd end on 45 + 20 = <u>65%</u>.

Triangular Graphs Show Percentages too — on *3 Axes*

Triangular graphs look terrible but they're actually fairly <u>easy</u> to use.

How to Read Triangular Graphs

Find the point you want on the graph.
<u>Turn the paper</u> so that one set of numbers is the <u>right way up</u>. Follow the lines <u>straight across</u> to that set of numbers, and write it down. Keep turning the paper round for <u>each set</u> of numbers.
<u>Double-check</u> that the numbers you've written down add up to 100%.
EXAMPLE:
The red point shows a population where <u>50%</u> are aged under 30, <u>30%</u> are aged 30-60, and <u>20%</u> are aged over 60. Double-check they add up to 100%: 50 + 30 + 20 = 100%.

How to Fill in Triangular Graphs

Start with <u>one set</u> of numbers — <u>turn the paper round</u> till they're the right way up. Find the number you want, then draw a <u>faint pencil line</u> straight across.
Do the same for the other sets of numbers, <u>turning the paper round</u> each time.
Where your three lines <u>meet</u>, draw a <u>dot</u>.
<u>Double-check</u> your dot's in the right place.

EXAM TIP

Triangular graphs don't crop up very often. If you get one in the exam the secret is to <u>turn the paper round</u> each time you read a different axis.

FACT

One of the most common uses of triangular graphs is to show the percentages of sand, silt and clay in soil.

**Section Five
Geographical Skills**

Types of Graphs and Charts

Two completely different types of map here
— topological maps and proportional symbols.

Topological Maps show how to get from Place to Place

Topological maps like this one show transport connections.
They're often used to explain rail and underground networks.

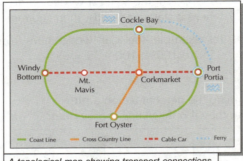

A topological map showing transport connections

> **EXAM TIP**
>
> If you've got a topological map in front of you, make sure you check out the key — it contains all the information you need to understand what the map is showing.

It's highly unlikely you'll have to draw a topological map.
If you have to read a topological map just remember the
dots are places. The lines show routes between the places.
If two lines cross at a dot then it's a place where you
can switch from one route to another.

Proportional Symbols Represent Different Amounts

Proportional arrows show flows or movement — the bigger the arrow the greater the flow. They're often used to show the movement of goods or people.

EXAMPLE:

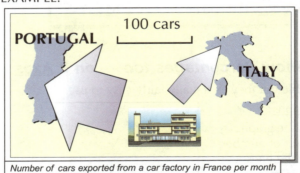

Number of cars exported from a car factory in France per month

Q: *How many cars are exported to Portugal per month?*

The scale shows that 1 cm equals 50 cars. The arrow pointing to Portugal is 1.5 cm wide. From this you can work out that 75 cars are exported to Portugal per month.

> **EXAM TIP**
>
> You need to be really accurate using your ruler for questions like this — there might be only a few mm difference between different arrows. If you don't measure them accurately you won't be able to answer the question.

Proportional circles are used to show numbers in different places on a map.
They're often used to show the population sizes for different settlements.

EXAMPLE:

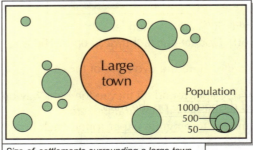

Size of settlements surrounding a large town

Q: *How many settlements with a population of less than 600 surround the large town?*

By looking at the key you can tell that the small and medium green circles show settlements with less than 600. If you count all the small and medium circles you get the answer which is 10.

Types of Graphs and Charts

**Section Five
Geographical Skills**

Isolines appear on lots of different maps in both human and physical geography.

Isolines Link Up Places with Something in Common

Isolines are lines on a map linking up all the places where something's the same.

Contour lines are isolines linking up places at the same altitude (see page 77 for more about contours).

Isobars on a synoptic chart (weather map) link together all the places where the atmospheric pressure is the same.

Isolines are flexible. They can be used to link up places where, say, average temperature, wind speed, rainfall, or pollution levels are the same.

KEY TERM

Isolines are sometimes called isopleths.

How to Read an Isoline Map

To read an isoline map you need to find the point you're being asked about. Then see which isolines the point lies on or between. You can then estimate the value for the place you're looking at.

It sounds pretty difficult but once you've seen a few examples it gets much easier:

EXAMPLE:

Q: Find the average annual rainfall in a) Port Portia, and b) Mt. Mavis.

Find Port Portia on the map.

It's not on a line so look at the numbers on the lines either side. They're 200 and 400. Port Portia's about halfway between, so the answer's 300 mm per year.

The question about Mt. Mavis is much easier. It's bang on the line so the answer's 1000 mm per year.

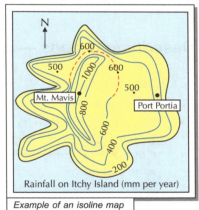

Example of an isoline map

How to Draw an Isoline

Drawing an isoline is like doing a dot-to-dot where you join up all the dots with the same numbers.

EXAMPLE:

Q: Complete on the map the line showing an average rainfall of 600 mm per year.

A: Find all the dots marked 600, and the half-finished line with 600 on it.

Draw a neat curvy line joining up the 600s and the two ends of the line.

Don't cross any other lines or go past the 500s.
The correct answer is shown as a red dashed line on the map.

EXAM TIP

Remember to check the units of measurement if you're reading figures from an isoline graph.

Section Five
Geographical Skills

Types of Graphs and Charts

The last kind of map you need to know about is choropleth maps.
To get the hang of them all you need to do is be able to use a key.

In Exams Choropleth Maps have <u>Hatched Lines</u> and <u>Dots</u>

Instead of using colour coding, the maps in exams usually use <u>cross-hatched lines</u> and <u>dots</u> — because it's cheaper to print in black and white.

They're very straightforward to use, but all those lines can be <u>confusing</u>. When they ask you to talk about all the bits of the map with a <u>certain type of hatching</u>, look at the map carefully and put a <u>big tick</u> on each part with that hatching, to make them all <u>stand out</u>. Look at this example, where all the areas with over 200 people per km² have been ticked.

> **EXAM TIP**
> Choropleth maps are used a lot in both physical geography and human geography so it's worth getting your head around them.

People per km²
= 0 - 49
= 50 - 99
= 100 - 149
= 150 - 200
= 200 +

Example of a choropleth map

When they ask you to <u>complete</u> part of one of the maps,
first use the <u>key</u> to work out what type of shading you need.
Use a <u>ruler</u> to draw in the lines, using the same <u>angle</u> and <u>spacing</u> as in the key.

Describing Graphs — Look for the <u>Important Bits</u>

The phrase 'Describe what is shown by the graph' is pretty alarming.
It's a <u>nasty looking</u> question, but what they actually want you to <u>do</u> is <u>easy</u>:

The <u>four</u> things to look for:
- Talk about bits where it's <u>going up</u>.
- Talk about where it's <u>going down</u>.
- If there's a <u>peak</u> (highest bit), write that down.
- If there's a <u>trough</u> (lowest bit), write that down.

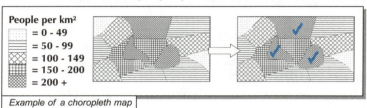
Important features on graphs

> **EXAM TIP**
> Using words like <u>peak</u>, <u>trough</u> and <u>correlation</u> to describe what graphs show will definitely impress the examiners.

Scatter Graphs are About <u>Best Fit Lines</u> and <u>Correlation</u>

With a bit of luck, any scatter graphs will already have a best fit line on them. If not, <u>sketch your own</u> in roughly the right place, then write down what type of <u>correlation</u> there is:

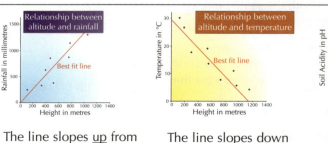

The line slopes <u>up</u> from <u>left to right</u> — there is a 'positive correlation'.

The line slopes <u>down</u> to the <u>right</u> — there's a 'negative correlation'.

When there's <u>no correlation</u> you can't draw a line of best fit.

The three main types of scatter graph

Revision Summary

Section Five
Geographical Skills

With this section more than any other, you need to do a lot of <u>practice</u>. Obviously you have to start by learning the <u>theory</u> of how to deal with maps and graphs, but the real test is whether you can do it for real in the <u>exam</u>. The best way to see whether you can do it is to try all these questions. When you've done them once, go back and learn any bits that you found tricky. Then do it all again.

1) Complete this compass to show all four compass directions:

2) Write down the four-figure and six-figure grid references of all of the symbols marked on the map that match the key.

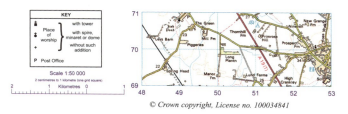
© Crown copyright, License no. 100034841

EXAM TIP

Don't worry if you're finding 6 figure grid references difficult — they're pretty tough. They get easier with a bit of practice. You can practice by looking up the grid references of places like your house and school on a map of your home area.

3) Using the above map, what is the distance, in km, in a straight line, from the post office to a) Manor Farm, b) Leys Barn, c) the nearest church?

4) Match each contour map with its corresponding shape.

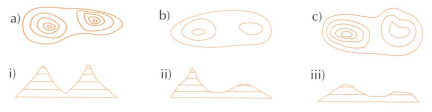

5) a) For each point A to D marked on the map below, write down whether the area is a gentle or steep slope.

   b) Give a brief definition of a spot height and a trig point, and give the six figure grid reference for an example of each on the map.

* © Crown copyright, License no. 100034841

6) From the map above, draw the lake and the outline of the forest (the black line). First, copy or trace the blank grid above, then measure some of the important distances to make sure you get things in the right place.

7) What kind of features would you use to work out how a photo matches a plan of the same area?

8) Describe briefly how you would work out what part of an area had changed and why, if you had a photo and a plan of the same area with different dates.

Section Five
Geographical Skills

Revision Summary

TIP
Go back to page 80-81 if you're having trouble with interpreting graphs.

9)

a) What sort of graph is this?

b) Describe the distribution of countries with an average life expectancy of i) less than 35, and ii) more than 51 years.

10)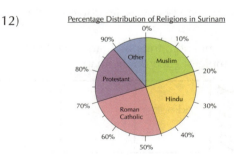

a) What type of graph is this?

b) Complete the graph to show the rural population dropped to 22.5% in 1990 and 19.8% in 2000.

c) In what year was the percentage population in urban areas at its lowest?

11)

a) What was the maximum temperature in Singapore?

b) Complete the graph to show that the maximum temperature in Nairobi was 16°C.

12)

a) What percentage of the population of Surinam is Hindu?

b) Explain in detail how you would draw a pie chart.

EXAM TIP
There's no denying that question 14 is hard. If you're stuck, remember the 4 things which are important to mention in graph questions:
- Talk about bits where it's <u>going up</u>.
- Talk about where it's <u>going down</u>.
- If there's a <u>peak</u> (highest bit), write that down.
- If there's a <u>trough</u> (lowest bit), write that down.

13)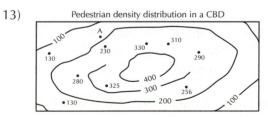

a) Complete the isoline for a pedestrian density of 300.

b) What is the approximate pedestrian density at point A?

14) Describe what each of the graphs shows in questions 9 to 12.

Key Terms

abrasion	The erosion caused by the scraping action of rocks, e.g. on river beds and banks, on cliffs.	**corrasion**	The erosion caused by the scraping action of rocks, e.g. on river beds and banks, on cliffs.
acid rain	Rain that contains a high level of pollutants. It has a pH of less than 5.6.	**correlation**	A relationship between two factors. Correlations can be seen on scatter graphs.
agribusiness	Farms run by large companies like McCain to make profit.	**corrosion**	The erosion of cliffs or rivers by chemicals in solution in the water.
alternative energy sources	Sources of energy that don't use fossil fuels (e.g. wave power).	**death rate**	The number of deaths per 1000 members of a population, per year.
arable farm	A farm that grows crops.	**deforestation**	The cutting down of large numbers of trees for wood or access.
arch	An archway in a cliff that has been formed by wave action.	**delta**	A bit of land made of sediment which sticks out into the sea at the mouth of a river.
attrition	A process in which rocks grind against each other in water to make smaller and smaller rock particles.	**dependants**	People of non-working age who are supported by the economically active members of a population.
basin	The area drained by one river and all its tributaries.	**deposition**	The dropping of material (sediment) e.g. by a river or the sea.
biodiversity	The number and distribution of different species of animals and plants.	**destructive wave**	A wave which takes material away from the shoreline.
birth rate	The number of live births per 1000 members of a population, per year.	**divergent margin**	A margin where tectonic plates are moving apart from each other.
central business district (CBD)	The middle of a city where land prices are high. It's mostly used for offices, shops and big public buildings.	**ecosystem**	The system of energy flows and interactions between all the living and non-living things in one place.
composite volcano	A volcano made from alternate layers of ash and lava.	**ecotourism**	Tourism where visitors are interested in protecting the environment and the lifestyles of local people. Ecotourism aims to be sustainable by minimising cultural and environmental impact.
constructive wave	A wave which deposits material like sand.	**epicentre**	The point on the earth's crust at the centre of an earthquake. It's directly above the focus.
convergent margin	A tectonic plate margin where two plates are colliding.		

Key Terms

evapotranspiration   Water lost to the atmosphere by evaporation (e.g. from lakes) and from plants giving out water in transpiration.

EU   Abbreviation for the European Union.

flood plain   The area of flat land that surrounds the lower parts of a river. It's made of sediment that has been deposited by flooding.

focus   The point within the earth's crust where an earthquake starts. It's directly below the epicentre.

footloose industries   Industries which don't need to be located near raw materials. Instead they often locate in pleasant surroundings and close to good communication links.

fossil fuels   Fuels like oil and coal that are non-renewable / non-sustainable.

global warming   The theory that the average global temperature is increasing because of increased levels of carbon dioxide in the atmosphere.

greenbelt   An area of countryside around a town or city where there are building restrictions. Greenbelts are designed to prevent urban sprawl.

Gross National Product (GNP)   The total value of all goods and services produced by one country in a year, including investments from foreign income. It's often shown per person (capita) to show how the wealth is distributed.

infant mortality rate   The number of babies that die before they are one year old per 1000 live births in a country each year.

irrigation   The artificial watering of land.

LEDC   A Less Economically Developed Country. They're also known as the 'third world' or 'developing countries'.

levees   Raised river banks made from coarse river load material that is deposited during flooding.

life expectancy   The average age people can expect to live to, in a particular country (it's often lower for men than women).

longshore drift   The lateral movement of material along a shore in a zig-zag pattern.

meander   A bend in a river, usually found in the middle and lower sections.

MEDC   A More Economically Developed Country. Also known as 'developed countries'.

national park   A protected area of outstanding national beauty. National parks are popular places for recreation and there are often conflicts over land use.

Newly Industrialised Countries (NICs)   A group of countries which have undergone rapid industrialisation since the 1960s. NICs have a lot of foreign investment from TNCs. Some are also known as Tiger Economies.

non-renewable resources   Resources which will eventually run out (like oil and coal).

pollution   The contamination of land, air or water with substances which harm ecosystems.

population density   The number of people in a certain area. It's usually measured per square kilometre.

Key Terms

population policies	Policies introduced by a country's government to try to control the size of the population (e.g. China's One Child Policy).	**sphere of influence**	The area from which people are attracted to a certain shop or town.
population pyramid	A diagram used to show the age and sex composition of a population.	**spit**	A long, thin ridge of sand or shingle that extends from a beach into the sea.
precipitation	The deposition of any form of water in the air onto the earth's surface (e.g. rain, hail and fog).	**stewardship**	Using resources responsibly so some are left and damage caused is minimal.
primary industries	The collection of raw materials from the earth. Examples of primary industries are mining and farming.	**subsistence farming**	Farming where the majority of the produce is for consumption by the farmer and his / her family.
pull factors	Factors which attract migrants to a place (e.g. good schools and jobs).	**suburbs**	Housing areas on the outskirts of a town or city.
push factors	Disadvantages of a place which force people to migrate to other areas (e.g. crime and unemployment).	**sustainable development**	Development which meets the needs of the present generation without compromising the ability of future generations to meet their own needs.
quaternary industries	Industries that are involved in research and product development.	**tectonic plates**	The huge plates which make up the earth's surface. They float on molten rock called the mantle. The places where tectonic plates meet are called margins or boundaries.
renewable resources	A natural resource that will never run out (e.g. wind power).	**tertiary industries**	Industries which supply services to people or other firms (e.g. nursing).
Richter Scale	The scale used to measure the strength of earthquakes.	**urbanisation**	The increase in the percentage of a population who live in urban areas.
science park	An attractive, landscaped business park. Hi-tech, footloose industries often locate in science parks. E.g. computing firms.	**watershed**	The boundary between two drainage basins.
secondary industries	Industries where the main activity is making products from raw materials (e.g. making crisps from potatoes).	**wave cut platform**	An area of flat rock that is exposed when there is a low tide. It's made when the sea erodes cliffs away.
shield volcano	A volcano made only from basic (alkaline) lava.		

Index

A
abrasion 8, 16
acid rain 71
active volcanoes 3
aerial photos 78
afforestation 14
air pollution 70
alternative energy sources 59
altitude 23
arable farming 48
arches 17
Argos 54
aridity 23
armour blocks 19
artificial drainage features 13
ash 3
atmosphere 6, 71, 72
attrition 8, 16

B
backwash 16
Bangladesh 15
bar charts 80
bars 18
beach nourishment 19
beaches 18
Belize 58
birth rate 27, 28
Blackpool 55
Blue Plan 73
branching channels 13
Brazil 7, 47, 66
Burgess 33

C
cabling 67
calorie intake 43
canopy layer 65
car parks 69
catalytic converters 71
catchment area 7
cattle ranches 65
caves 17
Central Business District (CBD) 33
central place theory 36
chalk 17
channel flow 6
chemical dumping 73
Chernobyl 70
China 30
choropleth maps 84
clay 9
cliffs 17
clouds 6
coal 23, 59, 60, 61
coastal beaches 13
coastal defences 20
coastal features 17
coastal plains 23
colonies 42
commercial farming 48, 49
Common Agricultural Policy (CAP) 50
compass points 76
composite volcanoes 3
concentric zone model 33
confluence 7
conservation 56
Consett 61
constructive waves 16
contour lines 83
contours 77
convergent margins 1
corrasion 8, 16
correlation 84
corrosion 8, 16
counter-urbanisation 37
culverts 13

D
dairy farming 54
dams 13
Dartmoor 69
death rate 27
deforestation 15, 66, 67
deltas 13
demographic terms 25
densely populated places 24
dependency ratio 26
deposition 9, 16, 18
describing photos 79
destructive waves 16
developed countries 42
developing countries 42
development 43, 59
development gap 42
development indices 43
distribution on maps 79
divergent margins 1
diversification 51
dome volcanoes 3
dominant plants 65
dormant volcanoes 3
dormitory villages 33, 37
drainage basin 7
dune stabilisation 19

E
earthquakes 1, 2, 4, 5
eastings 76
ecotourism 56, 58
economic issues / political influences 49
elderly dependants 26
emergency services 5
emigrant 29
employment 44
energy 59
energy consumption 43
energy production 60
environmentally sensitive areas (ESAs) 51
epicentre 2, 5
erosion 8, 9, 10, 11, 17, 19
erosional features 20
estuary 7
evaporation 6
evapotranspiration 6
extensive farming 48, 49
extinct volcanoes 3

F
farming 44, 48-51
flexible working hours 55
flood damage 12
flood plain 11
flood zones 14
fold mountains 1
food chains 70
food mountains 50
footloose industries 45
formal sector 46
fossil fuels 59

G
gabions 19
game parks 56, 58
Germany 29, 30
glaciers 72
Glasgow 33, 38
global warming 14, 72
gorge 10
government 45
greenbelts 34
greenhouse effect 70, 72
greenhouse gases 72
grid references 76
Gross Domestic Product (GDP) 43

Index

Gross National Product (GNP) 42, 43
groundwater flow 6
groynes 19, 20

H
hard engineering 13, 19
hazard 4
headlands 17
headward erosion 9
hedgerows 50
HEP 13, 59, 66
hinterland 36
hobby farming 51
Holderness 20
holidays 51, 55-57, 58
honeypot areas 68, 69
horizontal transfer 6
housing 35
Hoyt 33
human resources 57
hydraulic action 8, 16
hydrological cycle 6

I
immigrants 29
indigenous cultures 57
industrial agglomeration 53
industrial location 45, 52, 53
Industrial Revolution 52, 72
infant mortality rate 25, 28, 43
infanticide 30
informal sector 46
information technology 37, 44, 45
infrastructure of cities 31
intensive farms 48
interlocking spurs 10
international migration 28, 29, 30
isoline maps 83
isolines 83

K
Kobe 5

L
labour supply 52
lagoon 18
Lake District 58, 68
land pollution 70
lateral erosion 9, 11
latosols 65
lava 3
LEDCs 25-28, 31, 32, 34, 39, 42, 43, 45-47, 49, 55-59, 72
leisure 55
leisure industry 55
levees 11
life expectancy 25, 43
limestone 17
line graphs 80
literacy rates 43
Liverpool, UK 34
local migration 29
logging 65-67
longshore drift 16, 18, 20
lower stage river 8, 11
lowland plains 23

M
magma 3
Malaysia 66
managed retreat 19
mantle 1
market 53
meanders 11
MEDCs 25-29, 31, 33-39, 42-45, 49, 57, 59
Mediterranean 73
migrant 29
migration 27-32
milk quotas 51
millionaire cities 31
mixed farms 48, 49
molten rock 3
monsoon rains 15
Mount St. Helens 5
mouth 7
multinationals 56

N
National Park Authority 68-69
national parks 56, 68, 69
natural disasters 42
natural regeneration 67
natural resources 57
New Delhi, India 39
new industrial estate 61
Newly Industrialised Countries (NICs) 46, 47
Nissan car firm 54
noise pollution 70
non-renewable resources 59
north-south divide 42
northern hemisphere 42
northings 76
Nottingham 38
nuclear power 59-60, 70

O
oil spillages 73
one child policy 30
optimum population 24
Ordnance Survey 76
Osaka 5, 34
out-of-town locations 36
overcrowding 32
overpopulation 24
ox-bow lakes 11

P
Pacific Rim 46
Paris 39
pastoral farming 48
Peak District 68
percolation 6
Peru 56
pests 50
photos 78
pie charts 81
planning regulations 68
plans 78
plate boundaries 1
plate tectonics 1, 5
plates 2
plunge pool 10
point bars 11
pollution 59, 70
population density 24
population dependency 26
population distribution 23
population growth 27, 28
population increase 31
population pyramids 25
population structure 25
precipitation 6, 7
primary industry 44
proportional circles 82

91

Index

proportional symbols 82
pull factors 29, 39
push factors 29, 39

Q

quarrying 64
quaternary industry 44
quotas 51

R

radioactive waste 70
rain forests 47
rainfall 49
raw materials 52
recreational lakes 13
refugees 28
regional migration 29
relief 49, 77
relief rainfall 49
removal of hedgerows 50
renewable energy sources 59, 60
renewable resources 59
replanting 67
research and development 44
reservoirs 13, 65
revetments 19
rice growing 54
Richter Scale 2
river basin 7
river cliffs 11
river energy 8
river erosion 8, 9
river pollution 70
river valleys 8, 23
rocks 17
ruler 76

rural-urban fringe 34, 51
rural-urban migration 31, 32

S

saltation 9
São Paulo, Brazil 32, 34
scatter graphs 84
science parks 45
sea deposition 18
sea erosion 17
sea pollution 70
sea walls 19
secondary industry 44
sector model 33
seismic waves 2
seismometer 2
selective logging 67
self-help schemes 32
service sector 45
set backs 19
set-aside 51
settlement hierarchy 36
sewage treatment plants 73
shanty towns 32
shield volcanoes 3
shoreline vegetation 19
six-figure grid references 76, 85
sketching maps 77
snowmelt 15
soft engineering 14, 19
solution 8, 9
source 7
southern hemisphere 42
sparsely populated places 24
sphere of influence 36

spits 18
spot height 77
stacks 17
storm beaches 18
storm hydrograph 12
subsidies 50
subsistence farming 48, 49
surface run-off 6
suspension 9
sustainable development 28
sustainable tourism 57, 58
synoptic chart 83

T

tectonic hazards 4
tectonics 1
tertiary industry 44
Third World 42
through flow 6
tombolos 18
topological maps 82
tourism 55-58
tourist development 56-57
tourist information centres 69
traction 9
traditional manufacturing 45
traffic congestion 35
transform margins 1
transpiration 6
transport 37, 53
transportation 9
triangular graphs 81
tributary 7
trigonometrical point 77

tropical cyclones 15
tropical rainforests 65
tundra 72
Turkey 30

U

underpopulation 24
urban land use 39
urban planning 38
urban population 43
urban regeneration 35, 38
urban sprawl 34
urban traffic management 38
urbanisation 15, 31

V

vertical erosion 9
vertical transfer 6
visual pollution 70
volcanoes 1, 3-5

W

walking trails 69
Washington, Sunderland 54
waterfalls 10
watershed 7
wave pounding 16
weathering 9
winding distances 76
world's wealth 42

Y

York 15
young dependants 26

Z

zoning 67